"Mercy! This book starts off grabbing you and does not let go. The inspiration that follows grips your heart and will transform you into a modern-day believer in the God who is more than enough. Have some broken dreams or circumstances that have just not turned out the way you thought they were supposed to? From experience I can say, 'Hang on! God is not finished yet with you, your life and His promises.' My dear friends Mahesh and Bonnie Chavda make the miraculous attainable for the everyday person and earth it out in amazing manner so you, too, can learn to make room for your miracle. This might just go down as one of my all-time favorite reads of my lifetime. Well done. Amazing indeed!"

—**James W. Goll**, founder, Encounters Network and
Prayer Storm International; author, *The Seer*,
Angelic Encounters, *The Lost Art of Intercession*,
The Coming Israel Awakening
and many others

"Mahesh and Bonnie Chavda spark faith. Their love for the Word of God and their commitment to the fullness of the expression of God's Kingdom consistently draw people—not to miracles but to the Miracle-worker. Since they write from a lifetime and lifestyle of passionately pursuing the Holy Spirit, you will be encouraged and challenged to believe for more of God in your life. You may be holding the seed of your miracle in your hands right now."

—**Reverend Robert Stearns**,
executive director, Eagles' Wings

"Mahesh and Bonnie Chavda are two of the most awesome Christians I know. I love who they are and whom they carry. Their amazing book *Make Room for Your Miracle* stirs up hunger for the presence of Jesus and for the courage to press in for our destinies. I pray that everyone who reads this book gets hit with a spirit of adoption and begins to soar in the fullness of all that the Father dreams for their lives."

—**Heidi Baker**, Ph.D., founding director, Iris Ministries, Inc.

"Mahesh and Bonnie Chavda's *Make Room for Your Miracle* is rich in wisdom. For those who are passionate about wanting more in their walk with God, it should be required reading. If you want to be used in miracles, signs and wonders, it is filled with examples of how to live so that the Lord can daily flow through you."

—**John Paul Jackson**, founder,
Streams Ministries International

Some are great teachers who reveal deeper truths that inspire you to live a unique and glorious life. Others live in the realm of supernatural exploits. The testimonies of those who walk in the miraculous inspire us to know that God is real and that the supernatural is attainable. Seldom do we find the combination of the two—great teachers who also live in the daily realm of the supernatural. But there are some. Mahesh and Bonnie Chavda represent that rare and beautiful exception at a time in history when the combination is most needed. *Make Room for Your Miracle* is an instruction guide for navigating into the realm where lifelong dreams can become living realities. Abounding with insight and vibrant with incident after incident of real-world overcoming and breakthrough, this book is a must-read for anyone who has had his or her cherished dream seemingly shattered or who longs to access a realm of sustained supernatural encounter with God. I consider the Chavdas my mentors."

—**Lance Wallnau**, founder, Lance Learning Group,
7M University

MAKE ROOM FOR
YOUR
MIRACLE

MAKE ROOM FOR
YOUR
MIRACLE

MAHESH & BONNIE
CHAVDA

Chosen

a division of Baker Publishing Group
Grand Rapids, Michigan

© 2009 by Mahesh Chavda and Bonnie Chavda

Published by Chosen Books
A division of Baker Publishing Group
P.O. Box 6287, Grand Rapids, MI 49516-6287
www.chosenbooks.com

Printed in the United States of America

All rights reserved. No part of this publication may be reproduced, stored in a retrieval system, or transmitted in any form or by any means—for example, electronic, photocopy, recording—without the prior written permission of the publisher. The only exception is brief quotations in printed reviews.

                    Library of Congress Cataloging-in-Publication Data
Chavda, Mahesh, 1946–
    Make room for your miracle / Mahesh & Bonnie Chavda.
        p. cm.
    ISBN 978-0-8007-9470-5 (pbk.)
    1. Bible. O. T. Kings, 2nd, IV—Criticism, interpretation, etc. 2. Elisha (Biblical prophet). 3. Shunammite woman (Biblical figure) 4. Miracles—Biblical teaching. 5. Dreams—Biblical teaching. I. Chavda, Bonnie. II. Title.
    BS1335.6.M5C43 2009
    222'.5406—dc22   2009022331

Unless otherwise noted, Scripture is taken from the New King James Version. Copyright © 1982 by Thomas Nelson, Inc. Used by permission. All rights reserved.

Scripture marked MESSAGE is taken from *The Message* by Eugene H. Peterson, copyright © 1993, 1994, 1995, 2000, 2001, 2002. Used by permission of NavPress Publishing Group. All rights reserved.

Scripture marked NASB is taken from the New American Standard Bible®, Copyright © 1960, 1962, 1963, 1968, 1971, 1972, 1973, 1975, 1977, 1995 by The Lockman Foundation. Used by permission.

Scripture marked NIV is taken from the HOLY BIBLE, NEW INTERNATIONAL VERSION®. NIV®. Copyright © 1973, 1978, 1984 by International Bible Society. Used by permission of Zondervan. All rights reserved.

Scripture marked KJV is taken from the King James Version of the Bible.

In keeping with biblical principles of creation stewardship, Baker Publishing Group advocates the responsible use of our natural resources. As a member of the Green Press Initiative, our company uses recycled paper when possible. The text paper of this book is comprised of 30% post-consumer waste.

For all the Shunammites we know, both men and women, whose faith brings to life again promises that seem to have died. In every place, your homes, your families, your churches and your nations, where you have built the room for God, may He come and make His habitation. May you see your children's children and find in every season that truly, "All is well!"

CONTENTS

FOREWORD

The experience of God in all His fullness transforms an individual regardless of the day in which that individual lives. While we can be taught about God and not change, we cannot *experience* God and not change. To experience God is to experience change. And multitudes in this hour are crying out for a direct experience with God.

The Gospel of the Kingdom, when preached and taught the way Jesus and the early Church did, is always accompanied by signs and wonders. The day in which we live raises many challenges concerning the impact and influence of the Kingdom of God on the culture. But if we hope to realize the full impact of the Kingdom on our culture, we cannot ignore that we need to both see and release the power of God.

Mahesh and Bonnie Chavda are no strangers to the workings of God and the operation and manifestation of His miracle-working power. They have taken the compassion of Christ to the nations over the years and seen firsthand what He can do when someone makes room for Him to move. Mahesh and Bonnie are committed to seeing multitudes immersed in the experience of God and His glory.

This powerful book gives you the opportunity to make room for the miraculous in your own life. Mahesh and Bonnie open up a world of possibilities as they open your heart to insights from the life of the Shunammite woman who made room for a move of God—and as a result made room for a miracle in her own life. She went from barrenness to birth and beyond. So will you, as you heed the insights and revelation from the volume you now hold in your hands!

We may be eager and ready to believe God for someone else to get a miracle. But when it comes to believing Him for a miracle for ourselves, we can find reasons coming up in our hearts and minds that convince us we are the exception to the rule. Mahesh and Bonnie will take you gently by the hand and lead you into the powerful processes of faith that make way for miracles to occur in your own life.

I deeply appreciate Mahesh and Bonnie because of their utter love and devotion to the proclamation of the Gospel in all its glory and power. They live passionately to see the glory of God manifest in the lives of all who seek Him. Once you embrace the notion that God has a miracle for you, a shift in awareness will begin to take place within you.

Robert Greenleaf, founder of the modern servant leadership movement, said, "One gets what one is ready for, what one is open to receive." Since God is a God of miracles, I want to suggest that the fact you picked up this book is no accident. Something inside you drew you to this significant treatise. Not only something inside you, but Someone greater than you has seen fit to prepare you for a life-changing encounter with miracle-working power.

I invite you to trust in the process God has been bringing you through at this time in your life. I also invite you to trust the two servants whom God has chosen to mentor you into an experience with His uncommon glory, and to prepare the soil of your heart for the miracle you need and deeply desire. A miracle is coming with your name on it.

My deepest thanks to Mahesh and Bonnie Chavda for their willingness to take us step by step on this journey of identity and destiny, and to unlock the secrets that pave the way for miracles to happen—to all of us.

Dr. Mark J. Chironna
Orlando, Florida

PREFACE

Behold, I stand at the door and knock. If
anyone hears My voice and opens the door, I
will come in to him and dine with him, and
he with Me.

Revelation 3:20

Three times in my life a knock at the door has had a profound
influence on me....

The first occurred nearly fifty years ago when I was fourteen
years old. My family lived in Kenya, Africa. I grew up in the
coastal city of Mombasa. We lived not far from the ocean, near
an old fort called Fort Jesus. The Portuguese trader Vasco da
Gama visited there some centuries ago. Now, the trade winds
would bring old sailing ships called *dhows* carrying dates from
Arabia and returning home with spices. The scent of bougainvil-
lea and the ocean wafted in as I opened the door, curious to see
who had knocked so softly.

There stood before me the figure of a young mother in Middle Eastern dress, a baby in her arms. She had the gentlest blue-gray eyes I had ever seen. This Arab woman was a refugee from Agadir in Morocco where, on February 29, 1960, a terrible earthquake took the lives of twenty thousand people. In those gentle eyes I could see pain, death and devastation. I do not know how that woman had made it all the way from Agadir to Mombasa, but she was there standing at our door, asking for help. She tried to communicate in Arabic, but I could only understand a handful of words. She kept repeating, "Agadir." My family brought out clothes and food and money. I know my family did all they could to assist that woman. She had learned the Swahili word for thank you: Asante. She kept saying, "Asante, asante, asante," as she walked away. I will always remember those gentle eyes. Her knock opened my heart to be tender to those in need.

About a year later, there was another knock on our door. I opened it to see standing before me a very pretty American lady. What could she possibly be doing so far from home, walking specifically in my neighborhood of Kibokoni in Mombasa, Kenya? She had captivating blue-green eyes. The eyes seemed to convey peace and victory. She wanted a glass of cold water, but she carried with her the message of eternal life. She and her husband were missionaries to Kenya. She left in my hands a New Testament, and from reading that book I came to know the Savior of the world, the precious Lamb of God, Jesus Christ. That knock on my door had profound destiny and completely changed my life. It gave me a future and a hope. Jesus had sent that woman to knock on the door of my heart. The Lord of Glory came in, and my life took a turn toward eternity.

Many years passed. And then one day, in a vision or dream or trance (I cannot say for sure), I heard, as it were, another knock. As I opened the door, it was as though a heavenly breeze blew toward me, and I saw clearly another woman in Middle Eastern dress, gentle and beautiful like the young mother from Agadir. She, too, had big blue-gray eyes. These eyes had seen pain and death, but they shone with resurrection glory. She stood at the door, studying me intently; then she smiled. "I am the Shunammite. I want you to tell my story." Something filled my heart— it was as if the river of life had just swept over me. This then is the story of the Shunammite, an amazing woman whom God called "great."

The Shunammite's story is one that the prophets recounted whenever they remembered the mighty acts the Lord God of Israel had done for His people. They had perhaps long forgotten the woman's name—or perhaps her story was so well known it was assumed that all who heard it were well acquainted with it, or perhaps the parts of her story that most inspired them were the miracles—whatever the case, the Holy Spirit remembered her. He prompted His spokesman many years later to recount her story. Jeremiah is credited with recording the Shunammite's testimony among the annals of Israel's kings. As Jeremiah labored over the fate of his people, the Shunammite remained a beacon of possibility and hope.

The book of Second Kings records the saga of the Shunammite— now a grown woman past childbearing years—as taking place within the twelve-year reign of Joram, son of apostate King Ahab and consummately wicked Queen Jezebel. Her recorded story follows Elisha's apprenticeship of some fourteen years to Israel's most flamboyant and compelling spiritual icon, the great prophet Elijah. After the dramatic reception of Elijah's mantle, Elisha heads the guild of prophets whose burden it is to steer the nation away from its headlong bent toward captivity.

In his first year of office he finds himself in Shunem as the houseguest of a nobleman and his wife. Then, while wrestling to avert his nation from certain disaster, Elisha becomes a shepherd to the house in Shunem. Between dealing with an apostate king, a murderous queen and heads of state of nations sworn to Israel's subjection and destruction, the man of God turns in to the house in Shunem for respite. That is when the miracles begin.

This Shunammite woman still speaks to us today. Hers is a story of recovery—recovery of promise, recovery of life and recovery of inheritance. Told here through the device of biblical fiction, as we imagine prayerfully the various day-to-day events of her life, her story gives counsel to everyone who has hoped and been disappointed, who has been obedient and unfulfilled, who has sown and is still waiting for a harvest.

Through her story the Shunammite bids you to make a permanent place of expectation where, in every season that comes, you welcome the God of miracles. Our desire is that her story told now will help you prepare room in your heart for God to make a permanent dwelling place. You will recover your life. You will recover your life's breath. You will recover your lost inheritance—permanent communion with Him. This is our prayer for you—to know the power and faithfulness of God toward those who remain faithful to Him. The Shunammite *still speaks* to us today. Let's listen to her story and make room for miracles.

Mahesh Chavda

INTRODUCTION

And it fell on a day, that Elisha passed to
Shunem, where was a great woman; and she
constrained him to eat bread. And so it was,
that as oft as he passed by, he turned in thither
to eat bread.

2 Kings 4:8, KJV

The Shunammite Speaks . . .

I was made famous by two of the most famous men in the history of the world: Elisha and Jeremiah the prophets. During a time when our nation turned to strange gods, my light shone in the darkness—a witness to Jehovah God. While the One who watches over Israel never slumbers, He also keeps His eye ever on the man or woman whose heart follows after Him. He will come to us like refreshing rain on dry land. And so we must believe even when nature fails us and hope tries to slip away. We must believe. We must hope. To lose hope is to lose freedom, to lose yourself.

My small world turned within a greater one. I was the daughter of devout parents who feared the Lord and served Him all their days. I learned my ways from a mother who was never idle—with her tongue or her hands. I discovered early that a person's intrinsic value was based entirely on one's ability to contribute in practical ways to the survival of the clan into which one was born. Daughters, at about age thirteen, were married out of the family, but generally within their tribal clan. The more beautiful in body and serene in spirit they were, the better the choice of a mate and, therefore, the better the family fared. Sons inherited their fathers' estates and brought wives—hopefully prolific ones— into the family, and so a son was twice as beneficial as a daughter. But that does not mean we daughters were loved less. I desired what is called a "meek and quiet" spirit because it pleased my father.

Do not imagine my life was an easy one though I was born to favor and influence. It was not wealth or influence that caused my story to be recorded in the holy Scriptures. My story is kept alive to help you learn to make a permanent place for the Lord and His anointing as I learned to do. I have waited long to speak. My testimony is a vibrant strand woven into the wide and beautiful tapestry of what it means to have faith in God.

Man or woman, old and young, you and I share the human condition. We all experience life, death, hope, despair, joy, sorrow, desire, rejection, belief and unbelief, fear and peace. And we share the search for that One who has the answers we seek. He is the same, yesterday, today and forever. Where He abides wholeness and well-being abide. In the midst of our circumstances, and sometimes because of them, God comes to work His great miracles. As He did for me, He can do for you. He is the God of miracles. You will find He is the answer to your deepest longings.

And We Listen . . .

The original intention of God for mankind has always been to create a permanent dwelling place for Himself. Jesus said,

> "Look at me. I stand at the door. I knock. If you hear me call and open the door, I'll come right in and sit down to supper with you. Conquerors will sit alongside me at the head table, just as I, having conquered, took the place of honor at the side of my Father. That's my gift to the conquerors!"
>
> Revelation 3:20, MESSAGE

When biblical narrative suddenly turns from a national event of deep and lasting impact, like the battle with Moab, to intimate detail of an unnamed woman from an obscure city in the Galilee, it shows us the Divine perspective. Set against the dark backdrop of national crisis and looming judgment, the prophet diverts suddenly to become a frequent guest of the house in Shunem. This story becomes an icon to the greatness of our God. And His greatness makes us great. Matters of a barren woman and the concerns of a king are equally significant to Him.

Whenever Elisha came knocking this great woman opened her door and gladly invited him into her home to rest. As she welcomed God's prophetic messenger, the Master came in with him. Elisha represents the double portion, miracles *plus*! He is the prophetic pre-type of Jesus, the High Priest of everyone who believes.

The Shunammite demonstrates a combination of character traits that make room for miracles. She looked well to the ways of her household, combining reverent simplicity and moral rectitude with warm domestic affections and earnest piety. She exercised "true religion." Yet she carried extraordinary confidence and authority, a kind of independence from unbelief, such that when her household was threatened she was undaunted and fearless. Not unlike Abishag from Shunem, who won the heart of King David, our Shunammite caught the attention of the Lord's messenger and captured the heart of God. When she most needed a demonstration of His hand, He gladly showed it.

We are about to uncover secrets of the faith that the Shunammite exercised to receive the gift of a great miracle. And when the gift was stolen this great woman pursued the Source of miracles and would not let Him go until she had recovered all. Her victory became the seed of more miracles. From resurrection to recovery to restitution, a heart of faith and relentless refusal to give in to difficulty made room for ongoing provision and a rich heritage for generations to come.

Do you have a hope, a dream, an impossibility that you long to be made possible? As you, like the Shunammite, make room for our miracle-working God, you make room for your miracle. Let's discover how.

1

AWAKENING DESTINY

Remember now your Creator in the days of
your youth, before the difficult days come, and
the years draw near when you say, "I have no
pleasure in them."

Ecclesiastes 12:1

The Shunammite Speaks . . .

Being born into a house in Israel in the Iron Age meant religion was a priority—everyone worshiped something and kept sacrosanct religious rituals. Everything one did from the moment of birth to the moment of death, like everything one did from sunrise to sunset, was influenced if not mandated by religion. Superstition and faith competed. For those of us who feared the one true God, the God of Abraham, Isaac and Jacob, remembering one's history, the workings of our God in the lives of our people, was key to maintaining our identity. Ours was the only God you could not see with your eyes. You had to look with eyes of faith for His footprints in order to follow.

I rarely saw a scroll inscribed with stories from the past. For our history to live, we depended on telling and retelling by holy men or clan fathers or, as in the case of my father, those who had learned it well from their own fathers and then told it to their children. Since we lived far from Jerusalem—a family's caravan could make the trip in two days—we generally depended on devout men to come to us, or we would go to them on certain holy days. It had been thus since King Solomon's realm divided into the Northern and Southern Kingdoms just half a century before my childhood.

King Jeroboam, who was crowned to lead the ten northern tribes that did not want further alliance with

King Solomon's progeny, built great bulls in Dan and Bethel to aid our people in worship. Father speculated that the king did not want anyone in his realm to return to Jerusalem for worship and perhaps gradually shift allegiance back to the royal line. We had no Levites in the north now. The prophets kept their residence in some of the cities in Ephraim, but they did not often turn in at Shunem. We would carry our gifts and offerings to the prophets at Carmel and hear them there. The journey took half a day's travel, west toward the great sea. As it has tended to do from before time began, faith toward Jehovah God created trouble even then.

My father was the patriarch of our compound and well respected in Shunem. He was the fount of our existence— though Grandmother and Mother were the water of his spring. It was his name we bore, his food we cooked, his house we kept, his family we held together and carried on. He had given us life and whenever life was taken away we recognized the preciousness of it all the more.

Those were days I got my first lessons in the politics of our nation, divided as it was. Just south of our pleasant little "island"—by that I mean the outcrop that was the compound of my father's house in Shunem—was another dwelling. The contrast was stark even to my young eye. Only an hour's ride by donkey, situated atop Jezreel like a pinnacle, was the opulent summer palace of King Ahab and his serpent-wife, Jezebel.

"Island of garbage." That's what her name meant in our language. What father would name his child so? A priest, no less! Obviously, as my father said, blind guides were leading the blind.

Father would spend the whole of our Shabbat with his mind on Jehovah God. It was our day of rest. With no chores to do, at least for the moment—for every child was incorporated into the family workforce at some level as soon as he was weaned—I loved sitting with him in the shade of our olive trees. They had grown from the cuttings that his father had carried back from Jerusalem when he traveled there for Sukkot years before. Our trees were by this time my father's age and had entered their prime for bearing oil. Shunem had its own olive and wine presses, and when harvest came the community worked together. It was always a time of great rejoicing. The streets were filled with the sounds of us children, playing and laughing.

The verdant trees spread their branches in the field behind our house—living testimony to the promise from Jehovah that the olive would flourish in our land. We used oil for everything. Oil for offerings. Oil for cooking. Oil for eating. Oil for light. Oil for healing cuts. Oil for softening our skin. Oil for life itself—all from these trees. I looked up into the low drifting limbs with their sprouts of thick dusty green leaves. Father was talking on this particular day about another kind of oil—holy anointing oil.

"What does *holy* mean, Father?"

"Consecrated to God. Set apart—like our people. Like our prophets and our Torah. Moses' face shone with holy anointing when he came down from the mountain with the tablets. It is the residue of the Presence of the Living One," he nodded at me, his eyes shining. "Words of life from the very mouth of God. Eventually the whole world will know. Just wait and see. Even the Gentiles will forget their idols and turn to the Lord."

"But Father, Gentiles?" I asked, incredulous. I knew they bowed down to ridiculous stone and wood carvings. As if a block of wood could answer their prayers! I had heard how Gentiles practiced the most horrible things and taught their children to do the same. I scowled at the thought. But I also knew that Gentile practices were making their way inch by nefarious inch into our own culture and religion. King Ahab was not the first ruler of our people to worship idols made by hands.

In fact, a succession of bad kings had ruled over our people from the days of King Jeroboam until now. It seemed impossible to imagine that with each new king Israel could degenerate spiritually one more handbreadth—but it did! Nadab, Baasha, Elah, Zimri, Omri and now Ahab. None of them righteous men like my father. Their names were like a poisoned nursery song. Baasha assassinated Nadab in order to be king, and that fate fell on his son Elah, who was assassinated. Dust to dust. Sow to the wind and reap the whirlwind, Father said. Zimri committed suicide, something absolutely forbidden for Jews to do. He burned himself inside his own palace so neither he nor his belongings would end up in the hands of his enemies. After him came Omri the divider when brother fought brother, the most shameful kind of war.

As the prophets foretold, that was the beginning of the end of the Glorious Land. It would be several thousand years later and take many thousands of entreaties to redeem God's people from their folly, but He would make good on His promise to plant them again in their land never to be uprooted. When that happened, Father said that it would astound and confound the wise men of the world. And it would happen in a single day.

"One day our people will have Jehovah for their king as He intended," Father told me. He was talking to me but seemed to be addressing the land itself as if to offer solace. "He thwarts the schemes of connivers, so that none of their plots come to fruition. He catches the proud in their conspiracies; all that intricate intrigue will be swept out with the trash!"

He poked his thumb in the direction of the palace and turned to look directly at me. "Suddenly they will be disoriented, and plunged into darkness. They will not see to put one foot in front of the other. But the downtrodden are saved by God, saved from the murderous plots, saved from the iron fist." He paused. "And so the poor continue to hope, while injustice is bound and gagged." He patted my hand on his arm. "It won't last forever. Moses is our prophet, and when he laid his hands on Joshua that holy oil began to flow. It continues to this day."

It seemed a hush fell over our garden in the afternoon sun as though the trees and the birds and the earth and sky were all listening to his words.

"Here." Father reached up one of his thick fingers and pointed. "You see these round buds here?"

I nodded and looked intently at the small clusters of berries beneath thick leaves.

"Each of them an olive in a few months time, God willing!" he said. "And you must help me keep an eye out that the birds don't come and try to steal our harvest when it comes near time for picking."

"They often build their nests in these branches, Father," I said. "I've seen them. And the doves make their way here to get out of the afternoon heat. I hear their cooing to one another."

"Conspiring!" Father said. "They are talking to one another in their secret dove language. And with one red eye they are keeping watch on you. 'The little girl comes!' they are telling each other. 'Be careful not to look suspicious or she will run to tell her father that we are spying out the fruit of this olive tree for ourselves!'"

I was giggling by now, not fully aware in the joy of my father's presence of what was being instilled in my heart. Day by day my sense of who I was, my identity, was being poured into my very soul—just as the oil from these olives would soon flow into its appointed vessels under my father's watchful care. This knowledge of my identity as a child of the true King was providing the strength I would need one future day in order to rise up and overtake my enemy.

And We Listen . . .

Scripture tells us nothing of the early years of the Shunammite; this scene is one we might imagine from her young life. The influences of the Israelite faith in Jehovah would have laid the foundation for her faith in action. The Bible calls the Shunammite "great" (see 2 Kings 4:8, KJV). And we can assume she is one of the heroes in the faith hall of fame in Hebrews chapter 11 because she is one of the women of Israel who received her dead back to life. This was just one of the miracles in her life. What made her "great"? Why did God come to her and fulfill her deepest longings? Because she made room for the anointing. She welcomed His Presence to come and abide.

A lot of modern books talk about greatness, but greatness that matters is greatness in the eyes of God. All else, as the Bible says, is dust and dung. King David worshiped the Lord, saying, "Your gentleness has made me great" (Psalm 18:35, NKJV). The grandeur of God is the majestic simplicity of His grace, His condescension—His "gentleness," as David said. It reveals the nature of God as utterly humble and as one who comes down to intervene when we invite Him into our world. The cross of Christ is the ultimate demonstration of this greatness. And in our world God is looking to make His habitation in a heart that is fit for His Presence.

In the eyes of God, then, what is our greatest destiny or purpose? What makes us great? We learn from the Shunammite a number of things.

33

First, we are hungry for God. And as we stay hungry, we are open to God to speak to us. This is, in effect, making a welcome place for the third Person of the Godhead. The heart that is hungry for the true God will recognize and welcome the Holy Spirit.

A heart that is prideful will almost always miss the visitations of God—miraculous and "ordinary." It is the hungry people who draw His Presence. Blessed are the hungry people, Jesus said. In every time and every nation there are those who hunger and thirst for the true God, and nothing will satisfy them except that they be fulfilled by God Himself. And then, when they welcome the Holy Spirit, it is not just an act of religion: They have a place for Him to abide.

Another thing that makes us great in the eyes of God is our love for His Word. The great ones truly treasure the Bible. There was a missionary whose path we crossed who had worked extensively in India. She told of meeting a woman who owned only a portion of the Twenty-third Psalm. The missionary offered the woman a Bible, but she declined it, saying, "Oh! That is too much. I have lived my entire life on these few verses. They are so rich they satisfy me." A few lines of Scripture had filled this woman's well her whole life, and yet how many people own a copy of the whole Bible and simply neglect it? If that is the case with you, your heart has likely become fallow ground.

The next thing that makes us great is a desire to honor the true servants of God. Those who are notable in God's eyes honor the vessels that carry His Presence. This awareness starts in our local congregations. Do not let the enemy make you offended when God puts you in a body of believers. You might often hear people say, "I don't need pastors, I don't need elders, I don't need church leadership and I certainly don't need relationships with those 'sinners' in the church." Too often people separate themselves from a living church body at the drop of a hat, and then in the hour that they need the double-portion anointing it is not there because they have cut themselves off from the vessels through which God intended His anointing to flow.

One more thing makes us great: simplicity of needs. We are not always wanting more "things," because carnality does not satisfy. First Timothy 6:6 says, "Now godliness with contentment is great gain." As we find our contentment with the Person of miracles, out of that communion He drops His words and glory into our lives.

The Shunammite faced enormous loss in her life, yet she lived out these character qualities with dignity. Scripture tells us that with all of her wealth and position, she lacked the one thing she desired above all else: children. Barrenness was a poverty that could not be appeased by human will. She faced humiliation and inner devastation, and yet she was content. She had dreams and longings, but she also chose not to let resentment or bitterness reside in her heart over what she lacked. Thus, she was never lying to say, "All is well." She could trust her destiny because she was at peace in her true identity.

The seed for your miracle has been sown in your identity as a child of your heavenly Father. Our identity—past, present and future—is defined by the word of Someone greater than ourselves. As we enter communion with the Lord, making a place of rest in and for Him, worshiping Him, praising Him, we are transformed and become a conduit for the eternal Word to enter and redefine our temporal circumstances. We are transformed and become transmitters of the divine King and His glory to others.

In every neighborhood on earth, God wants Shunammites— men and women. Wherever you are, whether you are located in the Middle East or Europe, whether you are in North America or Africa, whether you are in India or Australia, we know that through Jesus Christ, His shed blood and the power of His Spirit you can welcome the atmosphere of His glory. Your life becomes His place to dwell. It is a life that is fulfilled, a life that is redemptive, a life that is experiencing miracles. A life that transmits His glory to others around you.

Who Am I and Why Am I Here?

In our day, the world does not lack for spirituality. Atheism is not cool anymore. Relativism is in. Multiculturalism is the new morality. Multiculturalism, essentially, is a spirit of humanism that wants to erase the clear lines of identity. Opinion polls guide many cultures rather than moral convictions. Somebody controls the world market, but most of us do not know who, and we seem to have very little say about it. Our generation is more medicated, stressed, dysfunctional, image-driven and fear-controlled than any generation in history. We believe we are what we eat. We are what we wear. We are what we tattoo on our bodies. We are what we drive. We are where we live.

In Acts 17, Paul is speaking to the great philosophers, the great influencers of his time in Athens. He has seen an altar there set up to someone called the Unknown God, and he says, "Listen, the one you are worshiping, the one whom you say you don't know, can be known. Let me declare Him to you, let me make it clear."

And then Paul explains, "He is not worshiped with men's hands as though He needed anything. He gives life to all and breath to all things. He has made from one blood every nation of men to dwell on all the face of the earth, and He has predetermined their appointed times"—for instance, today—"and the boundaries of their dwellings"—for instance, where you live—"so that they should seek the Lord in the hope they might grope for Him and lay hold of Him. He is not far from each one of us. In Him we live and move and have our being."

What is the purpose of this quest to discover our true identity? It is to acknowledge God as Father. This is what it means to be called human. In theological terms, it is called *Imago Dei*, the image of God. Found in Genesis 1:26–27 (the Hebrew is *b'tzelem elohim*), the term literally means "something cut out from or formed in the image of God Almighty."

There are four aspects for humans in this doctrine. One, we have a capacity to know, to reason and to make moral decisions. Two, we are called to operate as God's representatives on the earth by ruling over nature. Three, we have a capacity to mirror the unity within the Trinity by relating to God and other humans. And four, we are created to glorify God through making His character visible within the rest of creation. Only humans possess these qualities.

The Key to Your Identity

There was a very odd story we heard on the news about a man in England who died. When his will was read, his family and friends found that his last request was that he be cremated, mixed with fish food and scattered in the pond where he loved to fish. And then his friends were requested to go to the pond and catch the fish that ate their friend—and eat them. Eeek! That is confused thinking about identity, but it gives a little picture of the importance of knowing who we are.

And very simply put, we know who we are because He is I AM and we are in I AM. We discover ourselves as I AM opens the visible revelation of His character, of His nature. But most importantly as we lay hold of our adoption as His sons and His daughters, we take on His identity. The future of everyone who makes this journey rests not in the elements of the material world or the imaginations of men. It is the knowledge of God as Father that secures our destinies and makes room for His abiding Presence.

When Jesus went to the cross, He had you in mind. Remember: He thought of you before He made the world. His mission was to die. Mission accomplished. God the Holy Spirit descended to remain on Jesus when He was alive. After Jesus was baptized, showing His utter submission, His utter loss to His own identity to please the Father, the Bible says in the gospel of John that the people saw the Spirit descend in bodily form and remain on Him. Then in the tomb the Spirit came again and breathed resurrection life into that dead mouth. Psalm 29 says that "the voice of the LORD is powerful" (verse 4). "The God of glory thunders" (verse 3). "The voice of the LORD makes the deer give birth . . . and in His temple everyone says, 'Glory!'" (verse 9).

I, Bonnie, experienced Psalm 29 in my own life when I was pregnant with our fourth child. I had a complication called placenta previa centralis, had hemorrhaged the entire pregnancy and had died twice. Finally at 25 weeks, my placenta had died and fallen out, my water had broken and the chance of survival for the life that might be in my womb (doctors still had not found a heartbeat) was grim. They took me in to do an emergency C-section. But in that time of darkness God spoke to us and said that we would have a son, that we were to name him Aaron and that he would live and not die.

I was lying on that stretcher, and they were getting ready to put me out. Suddenly, another Man entered the room. He came and stood at the head of the stretcher. And His voice, not with the words of human language but in light waves and rays of power like lightning and thunder, came out of Him into me and hit my vocal cords. I heard myself tell my doctor, "I can have this baby naturally." And that voice moved through me and surrounded my womb. In a few seconds, I heard five tiny "mews"—like a newborn kitten. *Mew. Mew. Mew. Mew. Mew.*

I pointed my finger at my doctor and said, "It's a boy, isn't it?" He looked ghastly. The doctor did. He was holding death in his hands. I said, "His name is Aaron, and he will live and not die," and then I passed out.

Aaron did live. Today he is a university graduate, healthy and brilliant. The voice of the Lord is powerful. The God of glory thunders. He is the beginning and the end and everything in between. When we understand who we are and why we are here, we can begin to make room for His miracle-working Presence.

So who are you? You are an eternal child of God Almighty, Creator of heaven and earth. Why are you here? That you might seek and find Him and be fully conformed to His image. When you have Christ, you have the key to your identity. You have something worth living for because it is something worth dying for.

In the first chapter of John's gospel, Peter's brother has seen Jesus revealed as I AM. He runs to get his brother and says, "We have found Him whom we were seeking." When Jesus sees Peter He comments, "So, you're Simon, son of Jonah?"

With that question Jesus is basically saying to Peter, Do you know who you are? And then as though He were answering His own question, Jesus gives Peter a new name. But notice that in Peter's life from that point on he is called Simon Peter. It is not until the end of his life that Simon Peter finds himself in I AM and is called simply Peter.

There was a transformation of the man—his identity and his image. And we know the story of Peter's weakness. When Peter denied Jesus, he was not yet sure who he was. Maybe he also was not totally convinced of who God was. But Jesus said, "Oh, I have a plan for you! I am going to take that clay and mold it to be like Me, the Lamb who overcomes, who triumphs."

And when we see Peter at the end of his life, we know that he was willing to die for what he believed. Church tradition holds that Peter was crucified upside down. He did not want to be crucified in the same image as the Lord. He now knew he was Peter, the rock. He had found his identity in Christ when his enemies threatened to kill him; he was immovable.

There was a news report from California that a son of the highest Hamas leader in Gaza had found Christ. Yes, he had to flee his country, his family, his people. He had to leave the identity that had him covenanted with death. He was quoted as saying that this means a break with his father, but that he was praying that his father would also come to know the truth, to find Jesus.

Identity begins with fatherhood. Every soul is born into the identity of a corrupted father, Adam, and into a covenant with death. But Christ has come to break the covenant of death, bind us into God the Father and give us the Kingdom with an inheritance.

Would you be great in God's eyes? Then let the great I AM draw you to Himself like a little child and show you who you really are. Your quest begins here.

2

IS IT MY FAULT
THE DREAM DIED?

As they pass through the Valley of Baca, they
make it a place of springs; the autumn rains
also cover it with pools.

Psalm 84:6, NIV

The Shunammite Speaks . . .

One night my father made my dreams come true.

I stood on our rooftop one calm evening after sunset, leaning against the stone parapet that circled its perimeter. Our roof, like everything in our lives, had boundaries. Our Law prescribed a low wall around the roof so that you might not bring the guilt of bloodshed on your house if someone fell from that height.

I gazed out over many dwellings and the darkening countryside beyond. A few oil lamps flickered through windows. One watchman's lamp shone orange in a tower beyond the city gate, and another glowed in the vineyard along the outcrop. Overhead a silver sliver marked the beginning of a new month, rosh chodesh, the new moon. A wisp of a smile in the heavens, like the Creator winking from His lofty perch.

A hound yowled somewhere from the streets below, letting out a long lament calling for company. I sighed and sympathized with the lonely heart: I was sixteen and not yet betrothed. Most of the young women my age were already coddling their newborn infants.

Three years had passed since the celebration marking my coming of age. Mother had made me a beautiful new tunic of finely combed wool for the party—Mother and Aunt had spun and woven the wool themselves, working one after the other at the loom for the space of three months. Under their expert hands, the soft creamy wool had then been dyed an exquisite color—the deep violet of early morning just before the sky takes on the promise of dawn. They told me many times that this was the same dye used for the curtains of the Holy Place, a hue that comes from sea mollusks the Phoenicians use in their textiles. The extravagance was touching to me.

Mother had done the embroidery work on the collar, a beautiful mosaic patterned in ochre and red. Father had given her twelve silver coins as part of my dowry. The coins would be fastened onto my wedding veil and hang down just over the line of my brow.

Now the coins and the rest of my dowry were packed and waiting in silent tribute to my deepest longings and desires.

My fingers drummed the cool stone until the sound of Father's footsteps on the stair focused my wandering thoughts. He had taken supper elsewhere and was late returning.

"Good evening, daughter," Father said, approaching me.

I kissed him on both sides of his face.

"Good evening, Father," I said in turn.

We stood for a moment in silence. I sensed that he had something important to tell me, so I waited. Watchtowers winked at us here and there; a whip-poor-will called in the distance.

"The king is probably strolling around on his roof right now surveying his kingdom," he said, half to himself. "One of these days he or that wife of his will tumble from their roof without walls."

So that was where he had been. Discussing politics with the men in the city.

Father turned and looked at me, his dark eyes sparkling. Then he rubbed his hands together like a tax collector and said, "It's done."

My mind went blank. Done? Had I missed something?

"Done, Father?" I replied.

"I have taken care that your inheritance is secure. It is a good match, daughter. You will be married, soon."

I cleared my throat and caught my breath. I had waited so very long to hear those words, and now that it had happened I was gripped with uncertainty. He had chosen me a husband, and I had not a notion of who it was. He had never spoken to me once about it before this night.

What manner of husband had he chosen? Was he . . . ugly?

I knew I could depend on the kind of character he would have. Father was a wise and kindhearted man. He was also shrewd in business and not about to waste the estate he had built. All this would be mine as he so often reminded me. But all this and an ugly husband were another matter!

Dread stole over me. A dozen frightful images paraded before my eyes.

"Do I know him, Father?" My heart raced as though it were thumping its way right up my neck and would soon plop out. I imagined myself the daughter of Jepthah—my virginity sacrificed upon the altar of my father's oath. I briefly pictured myself spending the next weeks in mourning among my maiden friends, wandering about on the hills till the day of my doom.

It seemed a lifetime had passed before his answer came.

"Joktan, our neighbor, from my cousin's clan will be your husband. He has his own inheritance and is a fine farmer. A nobleman. You will have high standing among our people. Together with his land your sons will inherit well."

Joktan! The handsome widower who caught the eye of every maiden heart in Shunem.

My eyes went heavenward. I must have done something right.

While Father spoke on about good character and high standing, stars of happiness danced before my eyes.

And before the silvery smile of the moon had twice traversed the night sky, friends of the bridegroom lit the way for Joktan to come and take me from my father's house. As we stood under the *huppa* I shone with radiant womanhood. But as the words were said over us I confess that I grew more and more anxious. Behind my veil with its jingling coins I sent my eyes sideways to view my new husband; the regal head seemed now one of an aged stranger. The house on the other side of our wall, the house to which I was being carried that night, seemed as though it was on the other side of the world.

Influential persons paid homage and toasted our covenant. We received a pair of glazed jars with fitted lids, a linen coverlet, coin and a vermilion-patterned carpet from the East. The wedding guests ate and drank long after the bride and groom were carried home like heroes to begin their new life together.

But as the party rejoiced into the night I lay awake in a strange bed; Joktan slept beside me at last. I had thrown my whole heart into the decision to marry, but my comprehension of this new life suddenly seemed weak and frail. I prayed that God Almighty would calm my fearful heart.

The next morning I averted my eyes when the servants brought water for us to wash. The linen from the wedding bed was presented to my mother-in-law, and moments later I heard her trilling tongue announcing to the whole world that the marriage had been consummated and I had been a virgin.

After we broke fast I waited anxiously for my husband to go out as Father did every day. I would be left with the women and would find an excuse to visit Mother. I wanted desperately to go home. But Joktan did not go out. He stayed two days and nights hardly leaving my side and then Shabbat started. By the end of my first week of marriage I expected that I would have a protruding tummy.

And so did everyone else. A month passed. Then two. Their eyes were all watching me, the eyes of my mother-in-law and the household and all the members of our clan in Shunem. They were waiting for the news. News that I was pregnant. News that never came.

One year passed, and then two. Then another and another. I went from hope to impatience to anger.

Why was this happening to me?

Sometimes the small decisions are as important as the ones that seem great. The decision to take time for someone in need, the decision to put a little something aside when all the world is spending itself in a frenzy, the decision to believe when everything says liar.

There are some decisions that seem to be made for you. The want of a son, the urge to hold a daughter was my chief desire, but with all my strength I could not will it to happen. I was righteous by all the means I knew. I kept within our codes. We traveled to Carmel on the New Moon and Shabbat to present our offerings and hear the prophets, but still the certain blessing I longed for, that blessing that would confirm me as a wife and mother in Israel, did not come. My hope began to lag behind. It lagged so long that eventually I ceased even to turn and look for its outline on the horizon. My supreme desire had eluded me. So eventually I just left it back there and thought it had slipped away. More years passed. We made our bread and did our weaving, and I became a useful nobleman's wife except for one thing. The most important thing.

How does one cast away that part of one's own body that causes offense? My womb, that part of my self created by Jehovah, refused its own destiny. Self-loathing ceased to wrestle with anger. Shame ceased to lift its weeping head. The path of my longings led only to the Valley of Baca.

It became my settled state of mind that there was nothing in this world I could have done to change the fact that I was barren. I turned my grief outward in compassion for those who suffered. I especially pitied persons who were ostracized because of an infirmity.

That was all because of mine.

And We Listen . . .

Because of the completed work of Calvary, our view of wilderness experiences can be revolutionized. As God carries us through the wilderness, He does a work of transformation in our lives, healing us, tearing down old idols from our hearts, revealing our inheritance, ultimately removing everything that might block us from making room for the Source of miracles.

The Bible gives us a powerful "wilderness experience" story in the Exodus adventures of the children of Israel. They left Egypt behind. They had a wonderful deliverance. They had a great victory. And then God led them into the wilderness. Were they following the Lord? Yes. Did they miss the Lord? No. They were following the Lord. But they looked around and said, "Hey, guys, this looks like a wilderness. It feels like a wilderness. It *is* a wilderness!"

Now the children of Israel had been living for four hundred years as slaves—and they thought and spoke like slaves instead of thinking and speaking and believing like kings and priests of the living God. They did not understand their destiny.

So with them, as with us, God uses the wilderness experiences to give them revelation and bring them into their possession. Or let us put that another way: If the Lord loves you, He will allow you to go by the bitter pool.

And at that time, it hurts. For some it may be a painful marriage, or a hurtful separation or divorce. For some the bitter pool might be growing up with an alcoholic father who abused your mother or abused you. For some, the bitter pool might be a sickness your child has had. The temptation during these wilderness experiences is to become victims of bad theology. We might start to think: "If God loved me, this would never have happened." Don't fall into bad theology! Always, for every bitter pool, there is sweetening, there is healing. When the people of Israel increased their grumbling, Moses turned to the living God for help. God showed him a tree—probably a piece of wood—that Moses threw into the pool. Immediately the water was totally healed and those millions of people could drink.

Stand Fast in Your Decision

Wilderness? Bitter pool? Testing? Why should this be? In order to see our response. God wants to temper our faith. He wants to take that decision to follow Him and make it a foundation upon which to build something weighty. For that to happen, it must be tested. This willingness to let hope die is a journey that we call "faith beyond faith." Surface faith is not tested faith. It is only through trials that your roots are able to go deep. If you do not want to be challenged, your faith will have very shallow roots. And if you start allowing indecision to settle in, it will grow like a weed and choke out your faith. It will turn you from your decision, and it will turn you from your promise.

Abraham went out "not knowing." Now he knew that God had spoken and said, "Abraham, I'm calling you out of the land of your father into a land that you do not know, and I will make your descendants like the stars of the heaven." That promise was fulfilled in Isaac. So where did Ishmael come from? Abraham began to waver on his decision, and indecision settled in and he cooperated with Sarah's plan to bypass God's plan. Expect your decision to be tested once you have decided for the Lord.

Israel had a promise: You will eat from vineyards you have not planted; you will drink from wells you have not dug. But that first generation wavered when they stood on the threshold of their promise and died in the wilderness. God tested His people in the wilderness where no natural circumstance could provide. They had the opportunity there to understand and grow in their dependence on God and God alone.

Have you ever said, "I've given up all hope"? You can get to a place of hope, hope that is eternal, hope that is real, hope that is in Christ Jesus. You can get there. But the front door is often tribulation. Scripture says that God gives the valley of Achor (trouble) for a door of hope (see Hosea 2:15).

Jesus taught us this. He understood by revelation and the Scriptures who He was. Once He stepped forth publicly to embrace His calling of Messiah He was immediately led of the Spirit into the wilderness. He fasted for forty days and forty nights—went without everything. After this, He was hungry, and that is when temptation came. The temptation to quit is not going to come when we are fat and sassy! No, when our longings come in response to the call of God, the way is often through the wilderness.

This is the mystery of faith. We must be vulnerable to having our hopes dashed. The way of victory for Jesus was the crushing way of the cross. But because He was willing to drink from that bitter pool in order to taste the joy set before Him, we can believe that God will nourish us in our own wilderness experiences.

Israel had shoes that did not wear out, clothes that did not wear out. Their bread literally fell out of heaven every day. There were no vineyards; there were no plants growing things for them to eat. It was a barren, hot, dry land. So the Spirit of God hovered over them—the cloud that shielded them from the desert heat by day, and the pillar of fire that kept them warm at night. Everybody knows that in the desert it is hot in the daytime and cold at night. Impossible circumstances, but the Lamb provided. Those who responded in faith entered the Promised Land.

Testing is an essential part of God's preparations for His eternal helper—that Bride who will be with Him on the throne, who will stand with the Lamb in the midst of the seven lampstands, who will abide in that place of living revelation.

Thank God for the wilderness.

Pass On through the Valley

"As they pass through the Valley of Baca [weeping], they make it a place of springs; the autumn rains also cover it with pools" (Psalm 84:6, NIV). If you are part of God's people, you have to pass on occasions through the Valley of Baca, the place of tears. But you know what? It says *pass through*. It does not say you are going to camp there permanently. You do not have to stay there.

Sometimes we allow the pressure to cloud our vision, and we begin to doubt our destination in God. And when that happens we tend to try to settle down in the valley. Those who never choose the right perspective can be destroyed there by the enemy. Things will be over more quickly if we understand that this valley is a testing ground, and we are just passing through.

If you feel as though you just do not have the faith you need to keep moving presently in your life, then realize that "faith comes." How? The Bible says that faith comes by hearing and hearing, listening to, receiving, the Living Word of God (see Romans 10:17). It is the Living Word that pours into us this life of faith. You are part of a supernatural race, a sacred secret, hidden for generations past and now made manifest by the Spirit.

The Bible is like a mirror. You can look into it and, by His mercy, God will allow you to see the truth about yourself. Sometimes it looks good, sometimes not so good, but that is how it works. We like to say that the Bible reads us! The Author will peek over our shoulders and show those old traits, those old characteristics, that old nature, that old image of that old man who inherited corruption through our great, great, great, great, great-granddaddy and grandmamma, Adam and Eve. But it does not end there. His Word is living and active and full of power.

When we feel tiredness in our minds, when there is not much faith in our hearts, when we think we cannot go on, this Word is a supernatural tool of the precious Spirit of God to sanctify us, to wash us, to build us up, individually and together, into the perfect reflection of the glory of God Almighty Himself. That glory was seen in one man, in Jesus Christ. Why? Because He was God. He could not be anything other than Himself. Now He is making us like Him so that one day it will be as it was in the beginning. Mankind was created in the image, the thumbprint, the divine reflection of almighty God that we might ever be in ecstasy and communion and fellowship with Him.

Next Step: Intimacy

"Therefore, behold, I will allure her, will bring her into the wilderness, and speak comfort to her. I will give her her vineyards from there, and the Valley of Achor as a door of hope; she shall sing there, as in the days of her youth, as in the day when she came up from the land of Egypt. And it shall be, in that day," says the LORD, "that you will call Me 'My Husband,' and no longer call Me 'My Master.'"

Hosea 2:14–16

Scripture indicates that when you stay firm with your decision, and once you have passed through the wilderness experience, you will come to know Him intimately as a husband and wife come to know each other when they have married.

"Now hope does not disappoint, because the love of God has been poured out in our hearts by the Holy Spirit who was given to us" (Romans 5:5). Suddenly, in the place of hope beyond hope and faith beyond faith we step into a divine experience—that very intangible tangible: Jesus loves me; this I know.

This means that we rejoice when our dreams seem to die, when our longings stay just beyond the reach of our fingertips. We choose to "glory in tribulations, knowing that tribulation produces perseverance; and perseverance, character; and character, hope" (Romans 5:3–4). It is making us more and more like the One who poured out His blood in love for us.

Sanctification is progressive. You are growing in anointing and understanding. You are growing in Christlikeness. There are things in you that are being healed.

When you accepted the Lord Jesus Christ, you were transferred from the kingdom of darkness into the Kingdom of God, the kingdom of light and life. But you were not instantly perfected. Second Corinthians 3:18 says: "We all, with unveiled face, beholding as in a mirror the glory of the Lord, are being transformed into the same image from glory to glory, just as by the Spirit of the Lord." We are all being transformed. We have not made it yet.

There is a beautiful scene in Mark 1:40–42: A man with leprosy comes to Jesus, gets on his knees and says, "If You are willing, You can make me clean." Have you ever seen a leper? I, Mahesh, have seen many who came to my healing services in Africa. In certain parts of the world leprosy is still a factor. You look and see that fingers have fallen off, and there is just a nub. And then the feet basically become nubs; the nose, the ears have fallen off. It is just a horrendous disease.

Imagine for a moment this man who has been cast out from society, friends, family. Deformed, infectious, possibly missing his fingers and nose, he comes to Jesus and says, "Lord, You can make me clean." Filled with compassion, Jesus reaches out His hand and touches him. It may have been years since this man had felt human touch. Now God Himself has put His hand on him.

You may feel deformed like that man who needed Jesus' touch. *I have messed up. I did this. I didn't do that. My dream has died. It's over.* A lot of people look great on the outside, but inside they are filled with hurts. Whatever your guilt and grief, Jesus today is filled with compassion. He does not say, "Okay, you rascal. Your ears and fingers have fallen off because your rascality has come up as a stench to heaven." When we are lost in our hurts, we tend to think that is how God sees us. We need to bring those festering wounds to Calvary and let those bitter pools be healed. He does not upbraid. He reaches out and says, "I long to know you more intimately."

Change the Channel

Bonnie and I have tried to discipline ourselves never to focus on pain and hurt. One of my most precious sisters was killed in a horrible accident. Yet you seldom hear us talk about it unless it is in a redemptive way. Her funeral was the place where I determined that the seed buried that day was going to produce a thousandfold. And do you know what? That was the year I started going to Africa to minister. Since that time this ministry has brought more than a million souls to Jesus.

Another example is this: We told extensively in our book *Storm Warrior* (Chosen, 2008) how Bonnie's cowboy father was one of the great old-time sheriffs in New Mexico history and a great dad. He was murdered in his home, and the gunman was never brought to justice. But we do not hover over the tragedy. We learned that when those things happen you deal with them redemptively and then change the channel.

If you are hovering over that pain, that hurt, that abuse, that scam that you were a victim of, change the channel. John 5 tells the story of a paralyzed man who had sat by the healing waters of the pool of Bethesda for 38 years.

Jesus asks him if he wants to get well, and immediately you see where his weakness lies. He does not give a clear answer like, "Yes, sir! I want to walk!"

No, he starts whining. He lists all his excuses: "I'm all alone; I don't have anyone to help me; others have let me down; other people always get ahead of me; I don't have a chance." If you are in this mode where you are blaming others, you are like this man. And the Holy Spirit would tell us individually and as a church: Get over it. Get up, take your bed and be on your way. No more lying around; no more feeling sorry for ourselves.

First Samuel 30:1–6 tells how David and his men returned from battle to the city of Ziklag, only to find the city burned and the women and children taken captive. David's own wives had been carried off. Now not only was he distressed personally by what had happened, but the men started talk of stoning him! No one encouraged him. Everyone said, "It's his fault. Stone him!"

David had real cause to give up, but he had been anointed the next king over Israel. So he encouraged himself, rallied the men to go rescue their loved ones and their possessions—and in 72 hours he was king over Israel! In his darkest hour he encouraged himself in the Lord. He could have quit, but he did not give up, and in a matter of hours he walked into his destiny.

Some years later, King David faced another terrible trial when his son born to Bathsheba grew ill. David knew how to fast. He knew how to pray. If anyone could have gotten hold of God on behalf of an innocent child, David could have. But God is God. And for His own reasons He chose not to heal that little baby. The child did not get better; he died.

Now notice that David did not become bitter. He did not wallow in self-pity, proclaiming, "Why didn't God hear my cry? Why was my baby not healed? If there is anyone who brought the glory of God back to Israel, I am the one. The Tabernacle of glory is here. We worship God 24 hours a day. Why couldn't the glory of God heal my son? God, I thought You loved me. Why didn't You answer my prayers?"

No, David trusted God in the middle of his disappointment. He washed his face and moved on. And we have to learn to do the same thing. You may have been abused. Wash your face, move on. You may have been betrayed. Wash your face, move on. Perhaps someone stole your money, your inheritance. Wash your face, move on. You may have been molested, suffering deep hurts that cannot even be described. But know that you put yourself in your own penitentiary when you fail to move on. You have to get up, wash your face and seek the Giver of life.

Jesus was

> despised and rejected by men, a man of sorrows, and familiar with suffering. Like one from whom men hide their faces he was despised, and we esteemed him not. Surely he took up our infirmities and carried our sorrows, yet we considered him stricken by God, smitten by him, and afflicted. But he was pierced for

our transgressions, he was crushed for our iniquities; the punishment that brought us peace was upon him, and by his wounds we are healed.

Isaiah 53:3–5, NIV

Does Jesus understand your hurt, your failure, your wound? Yes. He went through this for you, and now His ministry is to pray for you. He believes you can get up and wash your face and move on. And when you see Him, He will make you forget you were ever devastated by trouble.

This is a day of salvation for us, a day of healing. If you have been carrying certain hurts, disappointments and wounds—perhaps for a while—then let God take you in His arms and heal them.

The Right Perspective

One of our students from our Bible college gave us wonderful insight. He was saying how he wanted to take hold of the fact that the deep things of God are simple enough for a child—something that we stress again and again in our teaching and preaching.

He said that he had been laboring and struggling with a complicated and difficult issue. One day he was in his prayer closet saying, "God, why aren't You helping me? Why have You left me alone to suffer like this?" That heart's cry led him to ponder Jesus' words from the cross: "My God, My God, why have You forsaken Me?"

It suddenly came to him in a way that he had never considered before that those words reveal how Jesus was fully man when He suffered and died for us. In that moment, full of the weakness and frailty of a man who had come to the end of his strength, Jesus cried out, "Why?" And when He did so, He asked every "Why, God?" that any one of us will ever face in our lives.

Our young friend taught us a great lesson that day. We can ask God who, what, when, where and how, but Jesus has already asked every why.

It is a common response to troubles to ask, "Why?" Consider that line of thought to be a "land" that you are best to stay away from. You do not have a passport to go to the "Land of 'Why?'" If you cross that border you will be arrested and detained indefinitely. Stay out. Get your mind off your problem and onto the favor of God. Choose to become less problem-minded and more glory-minded.

We cannot afford to be people of poor decisions or indecision. Indecision, in fact, is the worst decision you may ever make. Faith decisions in response to God's call will move heaven and earth to make blessing come your way.

Hudson Taylor said, "It does not matter how great the pressure. It matters only where pressure lies." When the pressure comes, does it come between you and God? Or is the pressure pressing you in closer to God? Let the pressure produce the character that God wants to produce in us all.

But this process begins with making the right decisions. Perseverance, character and hope are produced in us only when we choose the right perspective, the right attitude.

Forgiveness is a decision. Repentance is a decision. Wisdom is a decision. Obedience is a decision. Happiness is a decision. Health is a decision. Courage is a decision. Peace is a decision. Light is a decision. Love is a decision. Blessing is a decision. Provision is a decision. Life itself is a decision. The Word says, "Choose this day life or death, blessing or cursing" (see Deuteronomy 30:19).

Coming Through

Why do dreams die? Did we do something wrong? No, the Spirit is driving us into the wilderness of testing to deal with our flesh in order to deliver us from it and reform the priorities of our ideals. This gives us the opportunity to come out of the wilderness experiencing the power of the Holy Spirit, the glory zone!

So we want to unhook you from the voice that has been saying, "You failed. You missed it. You don't get it. What's wrong with you? It's your fault."

We want to loose you from that and say be hungry for His Presence. Make room for Him. He wants to fill the place you are preparing for Him. Look what He said in the gospel of John: "Don't let this throw you. You trust God, don't you? Trust me" (John 14:1, MESSAGE). If you believe in Him, the God of heaven has said not to let anything bother you. Don't be anxious about anything.

The heart humbled by trials is His dwelling place. Isaiah 40:3 talks about a voice crying in the wilderness, calling for us to prepare the way of the Lord. It is in the wilderness we make room for Him. If you are experiencing a dry time, then, in the desert, make a highway for our God. "Every valley shall be exalted and every mountain and hill brought low" (Isaiah 40:4). Arrogance and pride will never see Him. But the humble heart shall become a dwelling place for the Lofty One, the One who rules from heaven. When real visitation comes, it comes to the one who has humbled himself in the fear of the Lord. In matters of holy visitation the way up is down.

When Moses threw that tree into the bitter pool, he was exercising faith in the Lord of glory. Galatians 3 tells us that

> Christ hath redeemed us from the curse of the law, being made a
> curse for us: for it is written, Cursed is every one that hangeth on

a tree: That the blessing of Abraham might come on the Gentiles through Jesus Christ; that we might receive the promise of the Spirit through faith.

verses 13–14, KJV

When Moses took that tree, he was exercising faith in the Lord of glory who was going to come and hang on the cross. And by faith in the coming Messiah, Jesus Christ, the pool was healed. Sometimes we forget how much God the Father loves us. He loves you. Get that as a revelation. He loves you so much He allowed His Son to drip with blood.

So, what is your bitter pool? You will come through. And when you have, you can give to others the same comfort you have received.

3

A GUEST FOR DINNER

> What they were not told, they will see, and
> what they have not heard, they will under-
> stand.
>
> Isaiah 52:15, NIV

The Shunammite Speaks . . .

After two decades of marriage we were still without son or daughter. I worked hard to reign in my spirit and find peace in humiliation. I made myself the perfect wife in all the ways I could. I overcame my shame when meeting the eyes of other women who could drop children like a chicken laying eggs. I ceased to feel the guilt that I had let my husband down. I ceased to cringe at the disappointment my father would have felt had he lived to know I did not bear an heir to his estate. I ceased even to hope that Joktan's seed might fill my belly. And Joktan—who, in his kindness, never considered his legal right to divorce me—was growing old.

I lay hold of wisdom as she would come to me and did not let her go. I had a strong will, and I found peace at last—shalom, my mother's word. "All is well."

Then one day Elisha came to Shunem.

The laws of hospitality run deep in our culture. We have no inns, so travelers would sit by the city well or gate or in the open square and wait for an invitation. Any city that left a traveler to find his own shelter in a street corner or along an alleyway was one whose residents had no nobility. That city could be subject to a curse. Our hospitality was mostly, though, an act of human kindness. To share a cup and eat from the same table could bind men, families, even nations together. Covenants were cut at the board; peace was negotiated between enemies. There are many stories in Israel of the angel of the Lord guised as a stranger in our midst. Abraham, Gideon, Rahab all welcomed strangers, and the blessing of the Lord came down to dwell.

But my mind was not on entertaining that day.

I had just come from my weekly round of visiting widows of several poor families. Their trembling hands would take the *pithori* filled with olives and *lebne* or figs and the shawls we had woven from our wool. I was giving to my mother. I was feeding and clothing my grandmother and keeping them alive. I was remembering my own heritage, and my longing for God was fulfilled in my action.

As it was nearing the noontide, Joktan and his workers would be coming in from the field, and my maids would be making preparations for our meal. I passed the city gates to return home, nodding a greeting at the clan chiefs gathered there. Every matter of importance was conducted within this fort. Here a man could make an appeal for mercy and receive justice. Just beyond the entrance I entered the bustle of townsfolk mostly known to me and most of them related by some limb of our family tree. They moved with extra quickness because the evening would herald Shabbat and everything would come to a halt.

I was crossing the main square, my housemaid Rachel behind me, when I noticed him. The man and his servant were making their way along the thoroughfare that led away from the city well. His bearing caught my attention in the way that a whisper causes one to turn toward the speaker better to catch what is being said. He was politely wending his way upstream in the opposing flow of the foot traffic.

Looking back I see that I had had a soft quickening in that part that moves one to guidance before the mind is fully assisting. Perhaps you know it. For me it is like taking up a honeybee for a moment, clasping it in my palm and feeling the tiny wings buzzing against my skin. Deep calls to deep where logic and rationale do not comprehend at first. It is partially woman's intuition, perhaps, but more, I think, the strum of the finger of the Lord upon the strings of one's spirit. That unction turned me that day from my own business to that of the travelers making their way along Shunem's high street, and I found myself following.

I suppose I would have passed him over in a crowd. He was dressed in the ordinary garb of an Israelite, the *beged*, and his neatly trimmed beard showed the slightest gray along his jaw. His mostly bald pate was rimmed with neatly trimmed hair. One particular piece of clothing stood in contrast to his noble bearing: Over one arm was draped a roughly made garment of goat's hair, the kind of which the sprawling tents of desert herders are made. He looked to be my age.

With him was another stranger who appeared to be a serving man. He was smaller, younger. But it was his master's regal demeanor that caught my attention. I saw no baggage with them, just a walking staff and a skin for water.

The words fluttered within my belly: Invite them.

I did not think further. I approached the men and said, "Have you anything prepared, sirs?"

Perhaps startled that so straight an invitation had come from a woman walking out alone, the taller man stared at me a moment. The second man brightened.

I asked again, "Have you any place to rest or take your supper?"

"Thank you, lady, but we are going down to my city in the south," the master replied. "We shall sup there for Shabbat." He indicated the freshly wet skin of water his servant carried. "We had only stopped to refill our skin at your cistern. Our business here is finished, though I thank you for your kindness."

"Let it not be said strangers were not entertained in Shunem," I said. "Allow me to offer my table before Shabbat. It would be more bountiful with your presence, and we could receive a blessing."

The servant looked pleased at my insistence. His master adjusted the black hair coat and appeared to be adjusting his disposition toward my invitation as well.

I did not know why he hesitated. Perhaps my dress as a nobleman's wife was hindering him. It was not uncommon for noblemen to be in league with Israel's king, even in his pay. Joktan was generous, and I sported his jewelry in the custom of our married women. My nose ring was half a shekel of gold, and the bracelets on my wrists weighed ten.

I pressed my offer.

"You are both welcome," I said. "Rest at our house just until the heat of day passes. You will surely be home before the shofar."

He glanced through the gates as if calculating the delay.

"What do you think, Gehazi?" he said to his servant. "Shall we accept the lady and delay here in this city?"

Gehazi rubbed his slim belly.

"A compelling invitation, my lord," he said. "Food would certainly be welcome." An enthusiastic smile spread over his face. "We should not offend so gracious a hostess."

"We are pleased to receive you," I insisted. "It's just a short way and our table will be full. After you have been revived be on your way."

Tucking the end of his shirt into his leather belt, the man finally acquiesced.

"I suppose we are the servants of your urging," he said. "We thank you, mistress. My man and I will follow your lead."

"Welcome, sirs," I replied. "Welcome to Shunem and to the house of Joktan and our fathers."

Just as I spoke the words, others came to offer hospitality. With a smile I explained quickly that they were to be guests at Joktan's house. Their looks of disappointment caused me to feel as though I had gained some grand prize!

This guest was different from any other we had entertained. I was struck by his unpresuming nature even though he was knowledgeable about many things. We learned that his name was Elisha and he was from Abele-homa. He told us of his youth and that he came from a land and home not unlike ours. His father's clan had land holdings to the south and west along the Jordan River. Joktan knew of them.

The guest did not speak of a wife or sons and daughters, but he knew about farming and persuading the land to yield its strength beneath the plow and treader. The men became engrossed and animated comparing notes about seeding and plowing stock and angles and lengths of plow blades used on terraces in comparison to the open plain. They laughed until the conversation turned from soil to war.

Issachar's militia had gone with the tribes earlier in the season when our King Joram called a coalition to rein in Moab and bring back the tribute they paid into Israel's coffers under Ahab. Sons of Shunem were among the offended ranks who returned to tell of the terrible spectacle on the wall when Mesha sacrificed his son to end the siege. Our guest had been a witness when Jehovah opened springs beneath the desert and watered Israel's men and cattle.

I sat breathless listening until the man and his servant rose to leave. Gehazi gathered up the garments and skin of water lying near his feet. He took two or three more olives for his cheek. I handed Gehazi the food stuffs I had prepared for their journey and went down with the men to the courtyard. As our guest passed over the threshold into the afternoon, bright sunlight streamed in. But something much brighter than the sun seemed to flood our house that day. It was a Presence, a sense of fulfillment and hope in things unseen. And when the guests had gone it seemed to me Another lingered. And thus a day that began like any other would be the most important of my lifetime. It was *moed*, that special moment when time and destiny meet in a simple occasion to kiss the prayers of hope and patient obedience. Not that I believe you can buy a miracle with all the prayers of the saints or obedience of donkeys. But prayer and faithfulness will sustain you while you are waiting.

And We Listen...

The King James Version of the Bible tells us that the Shunammite "constrained" the great prophet to eat bread, that is, to come for dinner. Literally the word means *laid hold of him.* She basically reached out and took him by the arm and said, "You are coming with me, and I won't take no for an answer!" Something was compelling her to bring him into her house. Obviously hospitality was at work, but there was more. She was hungry for something that she discerned this man had.

As you read the story in the Bible you realize that the Shunammite did not know at first that this was one of the great prophets in Israel. Maybe she saw him at the city well; maybe she saw him at the marketplace. Before she knew his identity she discerned something of the glory that compelled her to invite Elisha home. So you see, she was not chasing after a "personality." She did not hear in advance that "the great prophet is coming to your city, and if you go to such and such a place at such and such a time you can meet God, too." No, she was doing what she normally did, which for an Israelite woman likely included benevolence in her town. It is clear that she was a woman who feared the Lord. She was going about her everyday business. As she was faithful and righteous and pious and believing God, her path crossed with that of a man in whom she discerned the Presence of the Holy One. And when she recognized that she acted.

You may find as well that your *kairos* moment comes out of just being faithful to do what is required or customary. As you are going about your business, God will cause your path to intersect

71

with His glory. When you step into that crossroad you will want to be able to discern it so you will know what to do. That is, after all, the point of being prophetic. When you understand the times and seasons you will know what to do within them.

Elisha and the Shunammite were both descended from Issachar. First Chronicles 12:32 tells us that "the sons of Issachar ... had understanding of the times, to know what Israel ought to do." These people were prophetic. They were not asleep at the wheel. This gifting is part of the reason that when she met him in town she discerned something. She did not know who he was at that point, but she did recognize the glory that resided in him and, with that discernment, she knew what to do.

What Is Discernment?

One day, out of nowhere, I, Mahesh, felt compelled to go speak a word to our daughter Anna, who was home studying. It was not a hurricane-force word; just a little nudge of the Holy Spirit. I said to her, "Anna, tomorrow don't drive Daddy's car to school. Drive your mommy's car."

She said, "Okay, Dad."

As she was driving the next day, she crossed an oil slick in the road, and the car crashed. It was a terrible crash; the whole car was crushed. But she was in a car that had air bags—my car, the one she usually drove to school, did not—and it saved her life. The Spirit had given me just a gentle nudge, and I was able to flow in it. And I thank God today that she was willing to listen to that discernment.

Discernment means "to recognize and distinguish between." Discerning of spirits is recognizing and distinguishing between spirits. But then there is discretion. The Hebrew word comes from a root that means "to plan or to plot." It is used of God in a positive sense. When God has given discernment, discretion is knowing what to do with it. Proverbs 2:11 says, "Discretion will preserve you; understanding will keep you." Like your own personal security detail, discretion and understanding are there for your protection to see that nothing harms you. By them you are able to be as Jesus advised: "harmless as the dove but as cunning as the serpent."

The ancient priests carried the Urim and Thummim over their hearts. Those stones represented the voice of the Lord resting on the heart of the believer.

Just as we have physical senses of seeing, smelling, tasting, touching and hearing, we have these same abilities in the spiritual realm. The Word says, "Taste and see that the LORD is good" (Psalm 34:8). Revelation 2:7 says, "He who has an ear, let him hear what the Spirit says to the churches." You might "smell" the presence of evil. God does not want us to ignore these senses.

Think of it this way. In the physical realm, a mom will choose meat for her family's dinner that is a good color and smells fresh. If the meat has rotted, she will notice it right away. The spiritual senses operate in much the same way as the physical senses. If something is not quite in sync with God, His nature, His Presence, you will be just as aware of that as you would rotten meat. Hebrews 5:14 speaks of developing the spiritual senses by using them. When you have grown in discernment, you really have to work hard to ignore some of the things you will sense! This helps us choose the good and not indulge in anything that comes from a perverted or dark spirit.

Some people shut the door on everything spiritual so that they are not susceptible to deception, but they will miss the good things that God is doing. We should be men and women of discernment—not for the sake of being judgmental or trying to "tell the future," but for the sake of fulfilling our call to be mature believers.

Discerning the Voice of the Lord

Discernment is not a skill that comes to us automatically. A lot of people tend to think that once they are born again they will hear God's voice automatically. No, we need to learn to recognize how God talks to us.

The Holy Spirit generally trains us through three particular means. The first is the means of Scripture. Some discernment can be achieved fairly easily as we grow in knowledge of His Word. If a person dresses as a witch and rides into your house on a broomstick, for instance, your discerner should be telling you that this is not of God. If a person says she has a prophecy for you and spreads out her Tarot cards on your table, you will not need extraordinary discernment to realize that would be evil in God's eyes. The Bible tells us to avoid these things.

Next, the Holy Spirit trains us through a developed sense of recognizing His Presence. It begins, quite simply, by listening. Isaiah 30:21 says, "Whether you turn to the right or to the left, your ears will hear a voice behind you, saying, 'This is the way; walk in it'" (NIV). If you are not listening, you will not know the way. God may speak in a still, small voice or by dreams or by visions or by someone who gives you a word.

If you think you have heard from the Lord, test it. The Lord will not contradict what He has said in His written Word. If a voice speaks something different, it is not His voice. He will always edify and build the Kingdom of God, save souls, comfort families.

You will find that the prophetic is often a corporate experience. By that we mean that individuals often see and hear in part.

When we come together and share what we hear from the Lord we receive a fuller picture.

Next, the Holy Spirit teaches us through increased godly character. When you hear a word from God, you next learn to obey. Every time you do what God has told you, you gain confidence for the next time. As you grow in maturity you will see more and more fruit. Then you become willing to go deeper.

This is not complicated or mysterious. In fact, sophistication tends to hinder true depth. Psalm 42:7 says that "deep calls unto deep." If you are one inch deep, there is very little deepness calling unto deepness. It will be surface to surface. If you stay there you will never go to the depths of the goodness and greatness and awesomeness of God. Plus, on the surface is where all the storms are. The deeper you are in God, the less you are affected by any storms out there.

It is important not to let your emotions override your discernment. The widow of Zarephath is a good example. God told Elijah that He had spoken to a widow and told her to feed him. So Elijah went to her and said, "Okay, give me that morsel of food."

She replied, "Who are you? I don't have anything."

Had God spoken to her? Sure. God Himself said, "I commanded her to feed you." But she had not heard Him. She was too focused on her own painful situation. In the end, at the prophet's insistence, she grudgingly obeyed and was able to receive her breakthrough.

Negative emotions can prevent you from hearing the voice of the Lord. The more inward you get, the more you isolate yourself—even from God. That is why it is important to turn your attention to God through things like praise and worship. Choosing to focus on Him facilitates hearing the miracle word of God that will break open channels of glory and blessing for you and your family. God does not want to leave you alone. He wants to bless you and deliver you in your situation.

Beginning to Recognize the Presence

The Shunammite discerned that this was a holy man of God. What does it mean to be holy?

Holiness is the principal attribute of God. In God there is no mixture, no corruption. That river runs pure, and when you drink from it everything will live.

When it is God it is holy. Light and darkness cannot dwell together. In the clash of kingdoms there is the Spirit of the Lord and the spirit that is not of the Lord. The latter is what the Bible calls the Antichrist spirit. The word means "opposed to or in place of." Mixture is where you find the spirit of Antichrist. When it is Jesus, it will be holy.

Our aim is to welcome and stay in the atmosphere of the glory because that is the place where nothing is impossible with God. An example in our ministry was the resurrection of a six-year-old boy in the Congo. In the Presence of the glory I, Mahesh, received a specific word of knowledge. I said, "There is a man here. Your son died this morning. Come up. Today God is going to resurrect your son." When you give a prophetic word like that before forty thousand people, something better happen! And it did. In the glory nothing is impossible.

There are reasons why blessings come. Blessings are loosed because you welcome the Presence of God, you give room to the Presence of God. It is important, therefore, as God starts doing things—and we believe we are going to see Him doing more and more—that you start "touching" it. As you touch it, realize it is not you; it is His Presence doing it. In other words, don't get delusions of grandeur! It is like the scene in *Star Wars* when Luke Skywalker lets out a whoop after shooting down an enemy gunship. Han Solo calls out, "Great kid!" Then he turns and adds, "Don't get cocky."

It is good for us to do important work, but it is also important not to get arrogant because it is the Presence of God that is going to give us the victory; it is the Presence of God that is going to give us otherwise unexplainable deliverance.

And the other side is not to have a poverty mentality. This does not come automatically. We have to believe. Even though we have been delivered from slavery, sometimes people still think like slaves, and God has to deliver the heart of slavery from us, just as He did the children of Israel. We need to think like a royal priesthood, a holy nation. The King-Maker has adopted us into the kingly line.

It Starts with Visitation

It starts with visitation. You learn that when the Presence of glory "visits" you, He leaves blessing. He leaves refreshing. He leaves you better than you were before. When you get around the glory of God, when you get around the Presence of God, you and your family will always come out plus, plus, plus. Visitation is wonderful—but our goal is habitation. When we welcome and steward and nurture this coming of the Lord, we create the atmosphere for habitation. It is like saying, "God, if You are going anywhere, You are coming to my house!"

Think of the Shunammite. She said, "Man of God, if you are going anywhere, you are coming to my house. If you are going to eat anyplace, anywhere within five hundred miles of here, you are going to eat at my house. Would you like steak? Stroganoff? Chicken enchiladas?"

I, Mahesh, spent some time ministering in France, and my hosts said, "What do you like to eat?"

I said, "I like escargot."

Now, you might say *Yuck!* but I like escargot. So they fed me escargot every night. Those crawly things, you know? They crawl and they leave a trail. But when you cook them in garlic and parsley—yum!

So in a similar way, if we want His Presence to come we ask for it. We say, "God, I want it. I want it. I'm hungry for it."

This hunger is, we believe, opening the way for a new season in the Church. She has had a season of healing revival. There was a charismatic renewal. There was a prophetic movement. There was a time when the teachers came forth. We had the church growth movement. We had Toronto and we had Pensacola. But these were precursors to the manifestation of His Presence that we sense He is waiting to give. This is the season of the visitation, and those who are hungry for His glory will see miracles that we have never seen before. We sense it. We smell the storm and hear the sound of the abundance of rain. This is for us all. It is not for a few superstars. It is for every man and every woman. And the time is now.

As we receive the Presence our homes can become a colony of heaven on earth, and anyone who comes there will be blessed. Whatever you touch, whatever you lay hands on will be blessed.

I, Mahesh, remember in Cincinnati, Ohio, some time back during a healing service that a woman came up to me and said, "My best friend has cancer, and she's dying. Can you pray for her?"

I said, "Of course, honey. Where is your best friend?"

She said, "I brought her."

"So where is she?"

"She's outside."

I said, "Why do you keep her outside?"

She said, "My best friend is a dog."

There were five hundred people waiting in line. I said, "Bring your friend in."

So in a few minutes she came up to me with a big female German Shepherd, and I felt as though the Lord said, *Welcome her. She's a lady of My Kingdom.*

So I welcomed her. I said, "Hello, come here."

Her owner brought the dog up to me, and I put my hand over her. The moment I brought my hand over the dog, she fell over—slain in the Spirit. True. All of the pastors there were saying, "I've never seen a dog slain in the Spirit!" But God's glory was there for this woman and her sick dog. The Lord healed her friend!

If the atmosphere is there everything will be blessed, no matter what it is—your children are blessed, your business is blessed, even your dogs and cats are blessed. Something happens when you cultivate the atmosphere that welcomes the Presence. As you move in that authority, everything is going to come in line with the glory of the Lord—your life, your home, your marriage, your ministry. Everything has to bow to the name of Jesus Christ. And what you have been waiting for for forty years will come overnight. It will not be by your might, your power, but by the Presence coming to raise the dead, make the blind see, restore homes.

This is not just for you, it is for many households. In the coming days people are going to come to your house to say, "Can I find the glory here? Can I get a touch of it? My son is in prison, my daughter is on drugs—may I get a touch?" All because you discerned the Presence and welcomed the glory. This is visitation.

When I, Mahesh, was a young, poor, college student attending Texas Tech, I made my way to Dallas to go to a Bill Gothard seminar. I did not have two pennies to rub together, so I was thrilled when I happened to run into a family I knew from Lubbock in the midst of the huge crowd of people. They were staying at a friend's house and were kind enough to say that they were sure I would be welcome to join them. I could sleep on the floor or whatever. I was thrilled to have a place to stay and thoroughly expected to sleep on the floor somewhere for the week.

That night I went with them to what turned out to be a beautiful house. A lovely woman met us at the door. My friends introduced me and said, "This is our friend from India who is studying here in America right now. He needs a place to stay for the seminar. Can he sleep on the floor or the couch somewhere?"

The lady of the house looked straight at me and said, "No."

I thought, *O Lord! Talk about rejection!*

But she continued, "No, he's not going to sleep on the floor or on the couch. He is going to sleep in our master bedroom. My husband and I will sleep on the couch."

I tried to refuse to no avail. She told me that I could not stay if I did not use the master bedroom. So I thanked her very warmly.

Soon I was ushered to a large bedroom with its king-sized bed. I had never been in anything like it. I lay down and went to sleep just overwhelmed by God's provision for me.

Suddenly, at three o'clock in the morning a terrifying rushing sound woke me up. This was during the Vietnam War. Once I got oriented I realized that B-52 bombers were taking off from nearby Carswell Air Force Base in Ft. Worth. They kept taking off one after another for about an hour and a half. Everything was reverberating with that sound. The house shook, the walls shook, my bed was shaking. It was quite some time before I was able to go back to sleep.

In the morning, I got up and went to the kitchen in hopes of finding a cup of coffee before heading to the meeting. Instead, I was met by my hostess, who said, "I fixed breakfast for you."

I turned around and the entire table was filled with food: chicken fried steak, omelets, fried eggs, bacon, gravy, ham, sausage, all kinds of pastries, jams, jellies and fruit that I had never seen before. She said, "This is for you, we have already eaten." I was not sure what to think, but I sat down gratefully and ate what I could before going to the seminar for the day.

That night, the same thing happened. At three A.M. I was awakened by the jets taking off, and I lay awake under that tremendous roar until it finally stopped and I was able to go back to sleep. In the morning, my hostess again had prepared a tremendous feast. She said, "Yesterday we were out of kiwi, but I have some for you today." I would have never noticed. There was no way for me to eat all the food she had prepared. This continued the third, fourth and fifth day of the seminar.

On the last night, I again went to bed, but when I was awakened in the middle of the night this time I realized that Someone was in the room with me. Golden beams of light surrounded me. I have never seen such wondrous light. It was like living rainbows. It felt as though all the galaxies of the universe were with me in that room.

And in the center I saw Jesus. He had walked into my room. I was completely surrounded by His light and Presence. My breath was taken away; I was not sure whether I was dead or alive. If I was alive, I wanted to die because I did not ever want to be away from the absolute joy and ecstasy that I was experiencing. There is nothing in human language to describe the utter joy and delight of His Presence. I saw right there that light and love and truth are a Person, and His name is Jesus Christ.

Then, in the distance, I started hearing a symphony of musical instruments that I had never heard before. This music began to stir and play and reverberate all around me. I suddenly realized that the source was the sound of the B-52s taking off. But as those roars came into the Presence of the glory, each sound wave had to bow to the name of Jesus and was transformed into a song and glorious symphony praising the Lamb of God. That night a lot of my definitions changed because I realized it is all Jesus.

As morning light began to break at about 5:30 or so, the glory started collecting itself together, and the Lord started walking out of the room. I wanted Him to take me with Him. I did not want to be anywhere but in His Presence. And by the way, if you have a revelation of the glory, death of our earthly body has a whole new definition. Absent in the body; present with the Lord. There is nothing like the awesome glory of the Lord. But as the glory was gathering and the Lord was about to go, He turned and smiled and said, *I brought you to this house.* His eyes were so tender and full of love and compassion, and yet conveyed complete victory. He said, *This woman's husband has asked for a divorce, and she cried out to Me. I have put healing in your mouth for their marriage. As you speak, that word will heal them, and their marriage will be restored. I have put the anointing on you.* Then He withdrew.

I got ready and went to the kitchen. Again the table was laid out in a sumptuous feast fit for a king. I said to my hostess, "The Lord visited me last night."

She said, "I know." Then she said, "Several days ago my husband came to me after fourteen years of marriage and said he had found another woman and was leaving me. My heart broke, and I went into my closet and cried out to God. I have never cried like that, and I asked God to help me. For the first time in my life, I heard the audible voice of God. He said, *I will send My prophet to your home, and when he comes treat him as you would treat Me, and he will have healing for your home.*"

She was expecting me, and that was why she had laid out a feast every morning and given me her master bedroom. She had made room for the Lord to come and touch her and her household with her hospitality. She was preparing a place for her friend Jesus.

I did not come back to that region for nearly fifteen years. But when I did, I found that the Lord had completely healed their home and restored her marriage.

Her prayer in her time of desperate need made room for the miracle she needed and more. The visitation of glory that filled my room that night was a specific answer to her cry, and it left with me a permanent deposit of healing glory that has since brought healing to thousands of others whom I have ministered to around the world.

The Shunammite constrained Elisha to come because there was "something of God" about him. His presence in her home confirmed her discernment. She soon realized, as we will see in a moment, that she wanted that presence to abide there, and she made a place for him.

What a lesson for us as we seek to make room for our miracle! Our confidence must rest in the Hope of our salvation. His Presence must fill the place where we wait for His promise. As we are filled to overflowing with obedience, worship and service, as we desire above all else to make room for this Guest, we constrain Him to come!

4

BUILDING A HABITATION FOR GOD

"Be still, and know that I am God."

Psalm 46:10

The Shunammite Speaks . . .

After that first day, Elisha stayed at our house whenever he came to Shunem. I felt without knowing why that this was a holy man of God and made every effort to welcome him. As was the custom he and Gehazi slept on our roof if they came in pleasant weather. When it turned cold or rained we moved a servant from his quarter and gave that sleeping place to our guests. Our hospitality did not leave him wanting.

We still knew little of his business, really. Sometimes he was quiet and sometimes very talkative. He spoke of the nature of the world and the climate of things between Israel and Judah. Other times he recited proverbs or verses from our holy Law. Among the few belongings he carried with him were some scrolls with the ten words and scrolls of songs of David, which he would bring out and read. Sometimes he glowered, and I suspected that the court of Samaria lay behind his disfavor. But regardless of his burden he was always kind and thankful for every act of hospitality we showed. But do not think we were overly familiar. Though he soon seemed a member of our household, we had traditions in our culture and I was careful not to overstep them.

Joktan was sometimes rapt and interested when Elisha feasted with us, and sometimes nodding from a long day overseeing his estate. But I always sat at Elisha's feet catching every word as if it were the purest gold. I found that each time Elisha came I was being changed. Not since the days of being in my father's house had I felt so certain of Jehovah's grace.

I began to think we should make a steady place for them to stay. It would not be unusual, for in the days when the judges ruled our valley, houses hired the Levites and supported them with board and provision since they had no other heritage among the tribes.

I spoke with Joktan one evening about the idea, and he was pleased with it.

So it was settled.

We set laborers to work the very next day. While the construction was underway I visited the carpenter and ordered a fine bed and table with a chair rather than a simple stool. When the chamber was finished and the furniture set in place I had servants bring up our vermilion carpet, the wedding gift that had been hanging as a tapestry since our huppa. It would serve now as a floor covering, my final offering for the servant of the Lord of prayer.

Now you may not think that putting a man of God on the roof is much of an honor. But our roofs were exactly like their position: high. It was the place where families gathered as long as the weather was fine, which was most of the time in Israel. It was the center of most of our living. By establishing Elisha on our roof we were making our house his, putting him and his wants and needs center place.

When he came to us again the first time after the construction of the upper room, he was a man exhausted. He looked as though he had not slept for days. He was lean and drawn, and his step seemed labored as a man who wore his mantle heavily. Things had been difficult in Israel. King Joram's reign was evil. We suspected that our friend was often in Samaria as tensions between the north and south escalated after the war.

When I led him and his servant to the room I thought for a moment that the gesture, our gift, might move him to tears. Elisha looked at me with such kindness. It was a look of the grace my father used to give me when I knew I had done well.

"Even a carpet!" he said.

With a smile in my heart I said, "I'll send up water and have you some food prepared." And with that I excused myself and left the man of God and his servant to the restful quiet of the warm afternoon.

And We Listen . . .

Why did Elisha keep coming back? Because he could rest there. This was not a ministry stop for him; it was literally a refuge. He was not there to preach to her, he was not there to pray for her, he was not there to talk with her friends, he was not there to make everybody in town know that she was something special. That word *resting*—it is like the Holy Spirit settling on Jesus in the gospel of John when He came up from the baptismal waters. So the question becomes: Can we have a heart and a life where the Holy Spirit can come and be at rest? A place for His Spirit to descend and remain?

Mostly we get distracted from this goal by focusing on work, struggling in one way or the other. Sometimes it is from hyper-spirituality; sometimes we just miss it, like Martha. But there is real grace in letting the Lord rest. And that is one of the reasons this couple's relationship with Elisha evolved—he found a permanent place to rest. There is no way to tell whether or not Shunem was a regular stop for him prior to her running into him and constraining him to come home with her. But from that point, just as Jesus would go to Bethany and stay with Lazarus and his sisters, Elisha would go to Shunem.

But, at the same time, the Shunammite and her husband were not presumptuous regarding their guests' time and talents. The reason we know this, as we will see later, is that after he has come many times and wants to do something for her, he does not even know that she has no kids running around! We are talking serious rest for him.

Making room for a miracle means building a habitation for the Presence of God, being a reservoir for the glory. People are usually unable to relate to the Holy Spirit because they never allow Him to come and rest. They are always demanding—*give me, give me, give me*. This is a more childish approach, and the opposite of what He expects. He desires a place to rest.

How do we move from visitation to habitation? How do we cultivate the atmosphere of miracles? How do we keep it around us? The atmosphere determines the Presence of God, the breakthrough and the miracle provision. Here are four ways we have learned.

It Starts with Servanthood

The Shunammite was foremost a servant. She had no agenda. This was an attribute that Elisha would understand because he had learned it himself. It is how he came to have a double portion of the anointing of his mentor, Elijah.

Elisha's double portion goes back to the beginning when he was first called. First Kings 19:19 tells how the great prophet Elijah came along and called Elisha to the "ministry." Actually, Elijah never said he was calling the young man to the ministry. Elisha was going about his father's business, taking care of his father's fields like a good son, stewarding his own inheritance right there in his hometown on his father's property. This particular day he was plowing with twelve yoke of oxen.

Everybody knew who Elijah was; he was called "the troubler of Israel." So when Elijah came along and threw his mantle over you it was not exactly going to make you the most popular kid on the block. But that is what Elijah did: He threw his rough mantle over Elisha. The minute it happened, Elisha got excited. He probably said something like, "Oh! I'm the chosen one!

Well, thank you, sir, I had a feeling you needed a helper in your ministry. I'm ready to come alongside you; let's go to the nations. But, hang on, I need to take care of a little business at home—tell Mom and Dad, do a few things. . . ."

Elijah did not even break his stride. He did not go back to get his own mantle; he was on a mission from God. His reply was, "Go back again, for what have I done to you?" (verse 20).

At that moment, Elisha got the most prophetic revelation of his life and future ministry: He found out it was not about him. It was not about his priorities. It was not about his necessities. He realized that the anointing is going to cost you.

Elisha died that day of his calling. That is why he could get up every morning and serve a cranky old prophet. We can guarantee that Elijah never said to him, "Son, let's sit down over breakfast and you tell me what you dreamed last night." Elijah probably never asked Elisha's opinion about one single thing. He never said, "Here, let me show you my notes." No, he probably said, "Do this. Do that."

When Elijah was getting ready to be taken up, he and Elisha were on what we might call their last great preaching circuit (see 2 Kings 2:1–7). Elijah was going around to all the high places where Israel would gather in the regions, and at each stop the sons of the prophets would run out to Elisha and say, "Don't you know your master is going to be taken up today?"

And every single time Elisha would put down the luggage and look at the prophets and say, "Yeah, I know he's being taken, and I know what I'm supposed to do—keep carrying this luggage."

Elijah told Elisha to join those prophets: "Stay here," he would say. "Go join up with them. Establish your ministry center here: 'Elisha and the sons of the prophets.' Everyone will be coming to you."

And Elisha would answer him, "No, thank you. I've got to pack now. You're getting ready to go on." And he continued with him on the journey.

That really speaks to us about the nature of moving and developing in the anointing; you will never reach the destination. Or to put it another way, we should not let the destination be to establish a ministry where we are known for hearing the voice of God. That should not be the goal. The goal should be: I am here for the long haul. I am a servant of the Lord. What does He want me to do now? Reach out to my neighbors? Serve in children's church? Care for a widow? Paint my house? Often obedience in the mundane things is the bridge to our moment of encounter. Finally Elijah turned to Elisha and said, "Okay, what do you want?"

Elisha said, "I want a double portion of the Spirit that is on you."

"If you see me taken up, it will be yours," Elijah said.

Elisha was going to have to stay with him, serving him until Elijah literally was not there anymore, for the double portion to be released.

So if we want to make room for the anointing, we must never grow out of being just a simple servant of the Lord. There is no need to be in a frenzy, to feel compelled that somehow I must wake up hearing the voice of the Lord say something monumental. But maybe I got up this morning and I was thinking of that widow down the street, and how her screen door needs to be fixed, and how she needs somebody to pray that that pain of arthritis in her hands will leave her. That is servanthood that welcomes the Presence.

We are often grateful for the eighteen years that we stood by Brother Derek Prince, a senior apostle of the Lord, and served him. We never made demands on him. We reveled in every opportunity, small or great, to ease his needs, supply his wants—to let him rest and enjoy. For many years we cleaned his house for him. It was an honor for us to serve this man of God who was touching hundreds of thousands for God's glory. And you know what? In the day that we needed healing for our sons, the Holy Spirit was there. We sometimes wonder to what degree we were loosing the great anointing and blessings of God by serving and honoring the servant of God.

Jesus paid the price, and now we have a privilege of just walking in His footsteps. If it costs an arm here and a reputation there, then say hallelujah! We are just unloading baggage and making more room for the Presence.

Seek His Presence More than His Gifts

We have seen some unusual phenomena in recent years— waves of amazing and potentially confusing things. One of the things that we are observing is the difference between His gifts and His Presence. Which do we seek? His Presence.

Here is the thing. Romans 11:29 says that "the gifts and the calling of God are irrevocable" or "without repentance" in the King James Version. That means He does not take them back. These are divine, supernatural, anointing, equipping gifts, and they have His essence and power in them. We welcome all of them. They are for adorning His Bride.

Now the bride's dress is not the essential thing. Her jewelry is not the essential thing. The essential thing is the bride. The gifts are for her adorning; He gives them and He does not take them back.

But here is a mystery. Because God gives His gifts and does not take them back, a man or a woman can be walking in the flesh and can still use those gifts. This is why we sometimes see prominent ministers in big trouble. When the flesh begins to take over, God will come to us patiently year after year and say, "Let's work on this. Let's adjust this. No, let's not do things that way." But at a certain point if the flesh insists on having its own way—no matter how "religious" it is—the Holy Spirit can be grieved, and He will just quietly move away. When that happens, a vacuum is created, and you know the rule: Nature abhors a vacuum—the supernatural realm even more so. If the Holy Spirit moves back, another anointing can move in.

When the flesh is running things, the glory will move away. If God has given gifts the gifts will stay, but it is possible for them to get under another anointing. So for those of us who want just His glory, it is about something else. It is about having Him.

God is teaching us how to recognize His glory. We want to be a dwelling place for Him to come and rest, and eventually we will see the miracles from His Presence.

Allow God to Be Your Peace

The great miracles happen in the place of shalom—that place of peace, hope and wholeness where He can abide. Sometimes people disdain Jehovah Shalom in favor of other aspects of His Presence: "I want Jehovah Jireh! I want Jehovah Rapha! I want Jehovah Sabbaoth! Let Him provide for me; let Him heal me; let Him fight for me." They miss the point that allowing God to be our peace within allows Him to minister in all these other ways. We want Him to enter immediately into action when possibly we need to let Him come and rest.

"All is well," the Shunammite says. This is the Hebrew word *shalom*—wholeness, well-being, prosperous peace.

I, Bonnie, told earlier how the Lord had visited me prior to our son Aaron's birth. His voice literally traveled into my body and birthed Aaron in the presence of twenty or so intensive care workers according to the word of the Lord.

A few weeks later Mahesh was in Africa. Aaron, who was still no longer than my hand, was undergoing his fifth of an interminable number of major surgeries. I was feeling pretty sorry for myself that day—we had already faced death and death and death with his situation. I was tired mentally, I was tired spiritually and I was tired physically. I just could not sit still for another hour, so I went outside and stood under the portico of the hospital. It was a gray, rainy day.

I have always been careful about not being flippant with the Lord, but that day I leaned against a column of the portico and said, "Lord, if this is the way You treat Your friends. . ." Before I could say, "I sure don't want to be one of Your enemies," it was as if the eyes of my spirit opened and I saw Jesus standing there. He was leaning on the column across from me—just like an exact mirror image. He looked at me, and I heard these words clearly. He said, *Bonnie, I am here with you, and that is more than enough.*

I got a revelation of Psalm 23 that day. The Lord is my Shepherd. I shall not want. He was saying, "Shalom. I am here with you. Shalom. I am Jehovah Shalom." And He was. The circumstances continued to be turbulent, but that was a turning point. The situation did not make us lose our peace, and God ultimately brought Aaron into resurrection life.

The secret we learned that day was that the difficulties we had been through had actually strengthened something in us to be a dwelling place for the glory. We may be experiencing difficulties in this mortal flesh, times when we are really in need. But if we have made room for Jehovah Shalom to abide then it does not matter what the circumstances are. You can be in the lowest pit of hell, and in a moment your spirit man suddenly realizes that you are in His embrace. When that happens, nothing else matters anymore.

Keep an Eternal Perspective

As you make a place for God, He will reward you. He can reward you on earth, but your eternal reward is in heaven. This eternal reward has not been emphasized enough in the Church. There has been a lot of attention on the charismatic gifts—healing, miracles, provision for now—but we rarely focus enough on the fact that we are going to be rewarded in heaven.

We need to emphasize the comfort of this more and more. It will give us strength in days to come. When the greatest economy on earth is shaken, everything can be shaken. It is nothing to be afraid of. We need to pray that our eyes will turn to the Lord. And we need to talk about the heavenly as much as the earthly, if not much more so.

Why would the prophets have told the story of the Shunammite over and over again? Israel was facing one difficulty after another—famine, war, another famine, invasions. In the midst of these turbulent times this was a story about a person who had real peace. God became her peace. Jehovah Shalom could abide there.

That kind of habitation speaks of the crucified life and the satisfaction that comes from obedience to the will of God. He dances with us when we are in step with His plan and the glory and fullness of joy are present. There is ease in the glory. Making room for the Presence in our lives is the way we move from crisis to contentment. As we make a resting place for the Holy Spirit, He will descend and remain.

5

No Room for Compromise

In Him dwells all the fullness of the Godhead
bodily; and you are complete in Him.

Colossians 2:9–10

The Shunammite Speaks . . .

One evening when Elisha arrived at our door, he was more animated than I had ever seen him. We sat at table after the servants had gone to bed. The candle lights danced up the wall behind us, making shadows as if the figures of holy witnesses from beyond the veil listened to our conversation.

He finally told us of his mentor, the great Elijah, and of the days of his wrestling to bring Ahab's court and his Sidonian courtesan under the hand of the Lord. Elisha's hands waved in the air in dramatic illustration as he spoke of the confrontation on Carmel and of holy fire suddenly pooling above the altar and breaking open like some alabaster box come down off the brazier of God Himself to consume the sacrifice and throw Baal's priests upon their heads.

I sat with rapt attention, leaning forward, my elbows on the table, hearing him recount the miracles done at the hand of his master. The old prophet had called for drought as God pressed King Ahab to his knees. Seduced by his witch queen, Ahab had turned Samaria into a center of Baal worship.

"He did more to make the Lord God of Israel furious than all the kings before!" Elisha observed. "My master stood before Ahab in those days and made a solemn oath. I imagine him even now in my mind's eye as he strode into the court, his hair coat cinched tightly in his girdle." Elisha's eyes shone. "On legs like trunks of juniper trees he must have planted himself immovable before the thrones where Ahab and Jezebel reclined like lizards. He would have hooked his thumbs into that girdle and bellowed when the anointing came upon him. Sometimes he seemed to know his days were numbered on this earth and each one had its fill of trouble. He was like a charioteer driving furiously before the rain to reach the stronghold."

I longed to ask how it sounded when one hears the voice of the Lord as these men did. But I dared not break this spell of wonder over our table. The lights seemed to brighten as he talked on.

"In Ahab's time Hiel came down from Bethel and thought to rebuild Jericho, the ancient fortress where Joshua had prophesied that setting up that city's doors again would cost a man his firstborn."

Joktan spoke. "What a hateful legacy, erecting a stronghold that God had cursed. An insolent fool to build a city to his renown and by that act to die without sons to carry on his name."

When those words came from my husband, Joktan, whose wife had given him no sons, my skin flushed hot and I hoped the men did not notice.

"As the Lord God of Israel lives," Elisha went on, "I can see him now, eyes of fire, that bush of wiry hair sprouting from his head like a lion's mane." He changed his voice to imitate his formidable mentor. "There will be no dew or rain during the next few years unless I say so!"

He took a draught of his sweet wine. "And it was so," he continued, his voice again his own, as he sat his cup back on the table. "He was a true shepherd in Israel."

But then he told us of the tender side of Israel's greatest prophet, that the man had been very human. How he fled before the threats of Jezebel when she sought his life. How the word of the Lord had come—not in fire, or wind or earthquake, but as the soft voice of a gentle lover.

"Still and small but so full of certainty that it moved him from his hiding place," Elisha said. He looked up with an innocent face. "And that's when he came after me. Perhaps I should have fled that day!"

We laughed but knew there was sardonic truth in what he said. He took the anointing of the Lord as seriously as life and death itself.

"Imagine," I said at last. "Not even dew upon the grass according to his word!"

"'Three things only God Himself holds the key for,' is what he told me," Elisha remembered. "'Rain, children and resurrection of the dead.'"

And We Listen . . .

The spiritual and political climate of the Shunammite's times is reflective of much that we are experiencing today. Classically, the spirit of Jezebel or witchcraft is the forerunner of the spirit of Antichrist. It seems evident that this spirit of witchcraft is appearing in greater measure in the world, setting groundwork for the Antichrist spirit to come and lead societies and nations away from God.

As we make room for the Presence, we can rejoice in our position of victory in Christ in the great battle around us. But because it is a battle, we need to be alert to the strategies of the enemy. There is no neutrality in the spiritual realm. On one hand, as we have seen, God's Presence brings blessing, peace, miracles. But on the other hand, if we fail to make room for good, the door is opened to evil. The more that people shut the door on the anointing and the glory, the more they make room for the power of darkness to come in.

Here is a clear example. In the early years of the twentieth century, after the Azusa revival began to sweep like fire across the world, the major church authorities in Germany became offended by some of the expressions of revival. They actually wrote and signed a document rejecting this move of the Holy Spirit in their nation.

Essentially they told the Holy Spirit, "Don't come here." This created a vacuum in their hearts, which the enemy filled. That is how some of the most educated, cultured, artistic people in the world could massacre millions including children and think they were doing good. Since they rejected the move of the Holy Spirit, there was plenty of room for the spirit of witchcraft and the spirit of Antichrist to move in. The spirit of Antichrist was able to work so effectively because the power of the Holy Spirit was turned away.

The spirit of witchcraft, in ushering in the Antichrist spirit, seeks to accomplish three goals. First, intimidate. A classic example of this is rampant political correctness taking over the Western mindset. If that fails, then, second, manipulate. It looks for the places where someone can be seduced or drawn in. Third, if you will not cooperate through less overt means, the spirit of witchcraft will use force to dominate and control. These are some of the roots that are present in the clash of spiritual kingdoms evident today.

That Antichrist spirit is growing stronger. It is the spirit that calls good evil and evil good. It calls abortion a rational solution and labels as evil those who oppose the killing of babies. It calls alternate lifestyles normal and criticizes as judgmental those who uphold the biblical view of marriage. It includes spirits of racism, bigotry and anti-Semitism.

Most people do not realize that the spirit of Antichrist starts within the church. That means it can hide under a religious guise but will ultimately betray the truth. The book of 1 John describes this:

> Little children, it is the last hour; and as you have heard that the Antichrist is coming, even now many antichrists have come, by which we know that it is the last hour. They went out from us, but they were not of us; for if they had been of us, they would have continued with us.
>
> 1 John 2:18–19

We are seeing a lot of Antichrist doctrine, movements, cults, heresies, identity movements—different things that appear or claim to be Christian, while the fruit is anything but. The Antichrist spirit opposes the true anointing of Christ Jesus—Messiah, *Mashiach*, which means "the smeared One," indicating the thick Presence of the Spirit of God—and also opposes the anointing Christ gives to all of those who believe in Him and who have been washed in the blood.

The antidote to these evil spirits is to know who we are and why we are here. It is time for the Church to rise and shine!

The First Anarchy

The evil forces that are becoming more and more evident today have been at work for a long, long time. The battle started in the very first anarchy when that anointed cherub called Lucifer revolted against God's rule in heaven and sought to take the throne for himself. It was not a war with the usual weapons; Ezekiel 28 indicates that it was like a great political campaign of words (the Hebrew word for *trade* in verse 5 can also indicate a campaign of words).

If you think Satan is not beautiful and seductive, remember that he was able to convince one third of the holy angels—those beings that had been created as God's ministers—to join him in the revolt. That is the backdrop for the events occurring in the Garden of Eden. That fallen cherub was after humans, who were to be the heirs of creation together with the Son. It is hard to imagine that one created to be so logical could deceive himself into trying to usurp God.

But even before that original anarchy, there had been another council in the Godhead and, in advance, the Son had said, "I'll go down." Jesus met the devil face-to-face in the wilderness and laid him in the dust!

How did He do it? Jesus knew who He was, and He knew why He was there. There is power in agreement. Adam and Eve agreed with the seductive words of the serpent and gave him the kingdoms of the world. Jesus agreed with the eternal Word of God and broke through to victory, ultimately believing God's promises even unto death and the grave. And He came out victorious in resurrection power not only for Himself but for all who would become heirs of God through Him!

These are not myths or fables. These are not legends. These are spiritual realities that have impact on our lives day to day. When He opened His body on the tree at Calvary, Jesus spoiled those principalities and powers once and for all and put them under His feet. Though Satan knows that his time is almost up, he has refused to concede defeat, and so until Christ appears there will be war. Satan will go on deceiving as many as possible.

Compromise Opens the Door

Israel serves as a valuable example for us in just about all there is to learn about following God in the right way and in the wrong way. Within a few generations God's possession became corrupted by idols. Solomon cracked open the door by direct disobedience to a few simple boundaries God set in place. "Don't marry 'foreign' wives. Don't become enamored of the things Egypt loves, like fast horses"—the two things Solomon became famous for in his latter years as king of Judah. Those compromises corrupted his wisdom. His son Rehoboam took it to the next level. When the cup of God's wrath had filled He allowed a low-class fellow of dubious motive and character to be anointed as co-ruler over God's possession. It was as though the people empowered an image of themselves to reign over them.

Jeroboam set up the Northern Kingdom, and suddenly God's possession was split in two. The place where God had chosen to put His name, the Temple in Jerusalem, became an object of envy. Jeroboam built two golden calves and sat them at the gates of his Northern Kingdom. He copied the altars that were in the Temple. He made up new festivals, all to win the affection of the people. This way, he suggested, they would not have to make the long trip down to Jerusalem anymore. But there was a deeper agenda, and that was to keep himself in power: If the people went to Jerusalem, they might fall in love with God and, by association, the king of Judah, and he would lose his throne.

So you see, his plan was a substitute. Let's worship God, he said, but let's just do it more conveniently. Before long it was pure idolatry. The compromise that began a little at a time opened the door, and ultimately Jezebel waltzed through it. She was the daughter of a Sidonian priest, Ethbaal, a political alliance for Ahab when he became king of the northern tribes. She brought her idols and false religion and a deep hatred for the Lord and His servants when she came.

Knowing the Voice of True Power

We are seeing today some amazing spectacles of the spirit of witchcraft. And do you know what? The spirit of religion will tell you that you should be ashamed of yourself because you are not worshiping that thing that looks so religious. Maybe you are even starting to wonder if there is something wrong with you. Some are even wondering if they have lost their salvation. That is how powerful the deception can be.

You are not alone if you are feeling threatened by a Jezebel spirit. Just picture this for a moment. First Kings 19:1 says, "Ahab told Jezebel all that Elijah had done, also how he had executed all the prophets with the sword." This is just after that great encounter where the Spirit of the Lord came on His anointed one, Elijah, and fire came down from heaven to consume the holy sacrifice. Suddenly the masses got a revelation of the true God, and Elijah oversaw the deaths of the 450 prophets of Baal.

Jezebel was furious. She "sent a messenger to Elijah, saying, 'So let the gods do to me, and more also, if I do not make your life as the life of one of them by tomorrow about this time'" (1 Kings 19:2). In other words, "Elijah, you are a dead man." That was the spirit of witchcraft speaking. And when he heard that, "he arose and ran for his life" (verse 3).

Do you recall that King David fled for his life and hid in a cave? Elijah did the same. Here were two of the most anointed vessels of the Lord in history, and there was something that could make them run. It was the force that hates the Presence of Christ and anybody who carries that Presence. And friend, this is a reality in this world. If you are one of those anointed ones—in other words, are you a Christian?—then you have unseen forces working against you. Unfortunately, sometimes those forces can motivate "seen ones" who have one agenda: "If I cannot intimidate you and keep you controlled, then I will manipulate you and make you afraid, and keep you controlled that way. And if I cannot seduce you or make you afraid, I will make sure I dominate you with some kind of shackles that will keep you down and in place."

But that is not the voice of true power. The true power is the still, small voice, the Presence, His glory, Emmanuel, God with us. That is what we want to hear. David strengthened himself in that. Elijah wrapped himself in that like his mantle. Jesus heard it and said to Lucifer, "Man shall not live by bread alone, but by every word of God." We need to remember that divine conversation God had with us the day He called us. It is the still, small voice that speaks our true destiny and purpose in life.

Do you know that there is no cave so obscure, so hidden that you can fail to find God waiting for you when you get there? He will not allow you to be a cave dweller. He will not allow it because when you had that one-on-one encounter with Him, He put in you the heart of a valiant one, the heart of one who would die for the one who died for you. He loves that. It smells like the sweetest incense. It is the thing that makes His heart race. He is ardently in love with that little voice in you that said yes to Jesus one day.

Jesus gives life to the world. We are living in revival. We are living in an awakened sense. He is very near, and we are going to see His glory.

But you know what? Not everyone will go with you. That does not mean you are special. Rather it is the mercy of God if something in you is insatiably hungry for Jesus, if you want to make room for His Presence all the time. Your house is not empty. You are recognizing the anointing and discerning the glory. The glory is not necessarily some ecstatic manifestation of something unusual. The glory is that sweet, discernable, sure Presence of Holy God Himself, saturating us and leaving the sense that all is well.

Make Room for More of the Glory

What is the best strategy for opposing the Jezebel spirit and her consort, the Antichrist spirit? First, make room for more of the glory. Our weapon is the goodness of God. The glory is goodness. The glory is grace. The glory is mercy.

This Presence is for a great military strategy organized by the Captain of Armies, Jehovah Sabbaoth. Jesus Christ of Nazareth is coming down with His sword to lead His Bride into battle and into victory. First John 2:20 says this: "You have an anointing from the Holy One, and you know all things." So the answer, the Lord says, when the Antichrist spirit comes, is the anointing, the thick anointing Presence of the Holy Spirit.

The Word tells us that the last hour is approaching. "Little children," it says, "listen to the voice of the Spirit. Little children, receive your calling. Receive your anointing for the last days." You see, the still, small voice does not say, "Antichrist is coming! Quick! You had better make up some graphs and charts and a few more organizations so that you will be wise when that time comes."

No, it says "little children." It says that the more childlike you are, the more you are going to be able to flow in the anointing and in the glory of God. Let God arise. Let His enemies be scattered. Make room for Him in your heart. That is the best way to be equipped for the last epic battle against the power of Antichrist and witchcraft.

Close Off the Well

Paul admonishes us to work out our own salvation with fear and trembling (see Philippians 2:12). One of the ways we do this is to keep our hearts from darkness. Here is a way to help you picture this.

Suppose a demon comes along looking for a place to settle. Now suppose you have a pool of bitterness in your heart. It may be very small, but it is a bitter pool and is, therefore, a place that the demon can drink out of. A demon feeds on pain, and it will stick its little bucket down there as long as you give it access to drink out of your anger, bitterness, insecurity, jealousy, habitual sin, etc. It will keep drinking, and will call its buddies to come, and will ultimately set up shop and be dancing on your head.

The Lord is saying, "Keep your heart." Your spiritual health is determined by how well you choose to keep your heart free from these sins. As the Lord brings things to the surface, allow Him to deal with them—and show them no mercy. The Israelites were often told when conquering a new land to show no mercy. It is the same principle.

I, Bonnie, think that in my life, looking back, I often undertook a strategy of girding myself with an army of resources—prayer and fasting, disciplining myself, reading Scripture, getting support from outside, making battle plans against this stronghold to try to get victory in a certain area—when the simple thing would have been to go close off the well.

How do you do that? Look to the cross that sweetens every bitter pool. The cross is the highest reality. Through the cross Jesus spoiled the powers of darkness and delivered us from its bondage. Crucify the flesh and move forward into faith.

Remember, start with the *facts*: The Bible is our guide; our circumstances are not. Next move to *faith*, which believes and acts on the facts. Only then comes *feeling*. So instead of letting our emotions be pulled down into the mire of those bitter pools, we keep our hearts clean by basing our feelings on fact and faith rather than perception.

Enforce the Victory

There is an enemy. God wants us to be aware that a battle is being fought and there are principalities and powers with which we must contend. But if God is for us, who can be against us? We could paraphrase this to say, if God is for us, it does not matter who is against us. There is a battle being fought, but we are overcomers.

I, Mahesh, took part in a crusade in Brazil, outside of Rio, and several people told me with great concern of the big principalities and powers of witchcraft that had hold over that area. Did they think that would make me afraid? God had sent me. I was not going to be afraid of those things. Of course not. And we added names to the Lamb's Book of Life and saw some awesome miracles.

One woman, for instance, had been shot in the spine during a holdup in her store. Her spinal column had been traumatized, and she had been confined to a wheelchair for five years. She lived about nine hours from Rio by car, but her family flew her in. She had little kids, and when they saw me praying for their mom they started crying, having seen her paralyzed for five years.

I felt the glory and I said, "God is up to something, honey."

Well, I did not know what had happened because I flew back pretty soon after that. The Brazilian pastors brought me the report that she is now walking. She has to have a little help from a cane from time to time, but she is up and moving. If God is for us, who can be against us? We overcome by the blood of the Lamb and by the word of our testimony.

Colossians 2:15 says, "Having disarmed principalities and powers, He made a public spectacle of them, triumphing over them in it." Jesus triumphed over every principality, over every power. The war has already been won; we are enforcing the victory. Wherever we are, we are ambassadors of heaven and we enforce the victory of the Lord Jesus. Nothing can separate us from God's love and God's victory. That is the realm in which we live—the realm of victory and the realm of the Spirit.

As long as you are prepared for battle, never be afraid to fight. If God is for us, it does not matter who is against us.

6

Standing on the Threshold of a Miracle

> He heals the brokenhearted and binds up their wounds.
>
> Psalm 147:3

The Shunammite Speaks . . .

We had not seen Elisha since the new moon when we had gone to Carmel where he sat among the prophets. I now even more than Joktan took an interest in their preaching, and so I was always urging him to take me or send one of the servants with me. And we always took a gift.

The day began like any other. Bread-making, the soft thump-thud-thump-thud of the loom under the hand of the women in the household, a servant child's whine, the goats' bleating and the warmth of the brazier and open fire—all equally inviting. By that time we had twenty persons in our household besides my husband and myself.

The spring in our valley is a regal time. The rolling carpet of winter wheat and waves of wildflowers paint the landscape in broad swaths of color beneath our blossoming trees. Everything of spring is hope and life anew. The morning passed without event, and by midafternoon a lull had folded peacefully into the compound.

Elisha and Gehazi had arrived some hours before and taken the stairs to the upper room without a word. I was in the storehouse mixing spices for the stew we would have for our evening meal when I sensed a presence behind me.

"Mistress?" It was Gehazi.

I turned, only slightly startled. "Yes, Gehazi?"

"My master bids you come."

And so the two servants of Elisha— Gehazi and the Shunammite—went to the roof to wait on the man of God.

I paused under the shade of the trellis, maintaining respectful distance from the entrance to the prophet's room. Gehazi passed over the threshold and disappeared into shadow. I stood waiting and reached out absently to pick one or two wilting leaves from the tangle of vine upon the trellis. The roses filled the air with sweetness. The murmur of soft voices drifted from the room as Elisha gave his man instructions. I gazed contentedly over my Jezreel valley.

The wiry frame of Gehazi reappeared in the doorway, and he spoke to me.

"You have gone to much trouble for us, mistress," he said. "My master wishes you to know that your considerations have not gone unheeded." Gehazi nodded toward Elisha, whom I could see reclining upon his bed.

"He says, look now, after all this concern for us what is it he may do for you in return? Is there something for which he may intercede, perhaps with the king or his militia in these parts? The man of God would gladly represent you and your husband's request."

"Oh, thank you, but, no," I said. "As you can see we have need of little here. And as for the king's men, our clan inhabits this city fairly. I dwell among my own people. Please thank him for his kindness in thinking of us." I turned to go, and Gehazi retreated into the shadows once again.

I started down the stair and heard their voices behind me. My thoughts were returning to our meal preparations when Gehazi's voice called to me from above.

"Hold a moment, mistress," he said.

I turned on the stair.

"Please come," he motioned me back and across the roof once again.

This time I heard the voice of the prophet.

"Shunammite, come near to me," Elisha said.

I approached Elisha's door.

"Sir?" I said.

Out of the dim room Elisha spoke. "Come nearer."

Gehazi stepped aside and motioned me to the threshold. This was a place of intimacy with the man of God such as I had never experienced. Usually I was in the presence of Joktan or my maids or in the company of those who went to Carmel to hear him. His eyes intensified as he gazed upon me. The air around me changed. It felt like the crispness of a coming storm. He spoke abruptly.

"You have no children in this house?"

His words seemed to rumble through my being like silent thunder. A moment later the shock of the question seemed to fling me headlong back down that long dark valley, that place where anguish preys on unanswered prayers. All my past humiliation, the begging, hoping, questioning, denial and even rage came tumbling out of my heart.

My breath stuttered. "N-n . . ." I wondered why the word would not come out. I groped for the rest of it. "None of my own," I finally heard myself say.

They say a deep wound must heal from the inside out, else it will fester and the whole body will die of its infection. But I thought that to pursue such a healing would take more time and tinctures than one could possibly employ. How dare he open my deep wound

119

now so carelessly? He surely knew little of the misery his words caused, or he would not have spoken them.

"It shall be about this time next year," Elisha continued, "at the time of the spring lambing." I remember he paused. The sound of his voice seemed hardly to touch the surface of time and space around us.

"You shall embrace a son," he said at last.

A fire of emotion seared my face, leaving my cheeks burning.

What language was this? If those words had been spoken by any other man than this, our trusted guest, the compass of Israel in those days of darkness, perhaps I could have shielded myself from their piercing tips. Did he say it once or time after time?

Embrace a son . . . embrace a son . . . the words echoed. A son. The hope of my inheritance, the song of my heart once whispered in gentle expectation when I was young. A son. The sound reverberated off the canyon walls of my empty womb.

Liar! I wanted to shriek back. Deceiver! Yet it was the calm voice of one long dead with which I answered him.

"No, my lord!" I whispered. "Do not deceive me, sir." As I lowered my eyes I was weeping for my children who were not. I was Hannah. I was Rachel. I was every human who had failed at being.

I backed away and rushed from his room. The room we had built for him on our wall.

But Elisha did not see my shame. The prophet's limpid eyes seemed to be looking through me, and I would later learn that he gazed upon a babe, a boy, with eyes the color of dates like his mother's. A perfect son, fat and robust, with a head of curling dark hair, skin the color of honey. The tiny babe was suspended, swaddled there within my woman's form. Elisha could see him clearly.

I, however, fled down the stairs and into my bed-chamber, passing a housemaid who met me with a startled look. I—who was usually calm and at peace—charged past her as if being chased by Philistines with their spears. Once alone I buried my face in a soft linen pillow until my breath returned to normal.

Then, tired and spent, I rose and washed my face. Seeking at least cosmetic composure, I pulled the tangled strands of my wild hair back into my hair bands and redressed my eyes with softened lines of kohl to hide their crimson rims. I pinched my cheeks and brushed down the front of my tunic, straightening my belt and readjusting the folds of my skirt as I went out. Ignoring the back of my housemaid busying herself with her hand broom at the end of the hall, I descended the stair and entered the main floor, once again the collected mistress of my household. I crossed to the kitchen and resumed oversight of the preparation of my guests' evening meal as if nothing had happened.

At first I did not mention to Joktan or to anyone what the prophet had said. I laid the words aside. But in a few months' time they seemed no longer to taunt me. I gave them permission to come and settle down in my heart. "You shall embrace a son!" And one night as I drifted off to sleep beside my husband, I knew it would be.

One morning, not too long afterward, I awoke and rushed from my bed, my head reeling and my stomach heaving. I passed the first month, and that unpleasant-ness was more pleasant than any preoccupation I had

121

kept. I waited another month and when it was certain, I told Joktan that he was to be a father in his old age. Soon the word of it spread—that I, the Shunammite woman who had lived before her people in barrenness, lo, these many years, would embrace a son at last!

When the day came the midwife helped me upon the birthing stool. Beads of sweat poured down upon my brow as delirium and determination washed over me with every birth pang. With one final crashing effort a quarter century of prayers and looking to heaven bore fruit.

"A son!" the midwife exclaimed.

I gasped with relief then burst out in laughter and tears. At last I embraced my miracle. The one for which I had waited.

It became an ensign, our boy's birth. A sign that nothing was impossible for the God of Israel. Our miracle, the son Jehovah gave, was much talked about from Shunem down to Elisha's home city and back up to Carmel where the mountain overlooks the sea. In that same week, as providence would have it, we cut down our firstfruits and Joktan prepared the offering for our harvest to be presented before the Lord. We redeemed him as the Lord has said: "Consecrate to Me every first-born; man and beast, the first issue of every womb among the Israelites is Mine."

I kept the purification ritual, and after the *mikvah* I prepared myself for our son's entrance into the covenant of our fathers. On the eighth day after our son was born he was joined to the Lord in the covenant of Abraham by being circumcised according to the commandment. Joktan beamed with pride and pronounced his name in the presence of all for the first time: Habakkuk. It means "embrace."

After I had fulfilled the days of my purification and could ride I persuaded Joktan to take Habakkuk and me to Carmel to dedicate the son He had given. After that they became so accustomed to my face that any one of them could say "the Shunammite" and all the others knew it meant me.

The man of God and his servant came in the first month of our son's life. Elisha brought our boy a gift: a finely crafted box overlaid with beautiful filigreed work done by a silversmith in Jerusalem. It contained a scroll written by a scribe from the Temple.

Shema Yisrael Adonai elohenu Adonai echad.

Then the prophet recited the words of our fathers.

Joktan and I closed our eyes and drank in the blessing of the word of the Lord as Elisha pronounced them over us, our house and our son.

And We Listen . . .

When we have welcomed the Lord of glory, it is possible at any moment that our usual errands and chores will suddenly take us to that room of miracles where God has determined to come and rest.

Consider our story thus far. The man of God comes to town and meets a woman who compels him to share a meal at her house. He starts coming regularly because she treats him so well and does not demand anything from him. Then one day after a little while he is resting on his bed, and his conscience starts to strike him. He thinks, *You know, I have been eating this woman's food and enjoying her hospitality and—my gosh!—maybe she has a need.*

So he tells his servant to call her, and she comes and stands in the door. Elisha looks at her and, in the odd communication that prophets and their servants and people had in those days, he does not speak to her directly. He says to the servant, "Ask her what she needs." The servant says, "What do you need?" and the answer is, "Nothing."

"Hmm," says Elisha. "We have to do something for her."

So the servant says, "Well, Mr. Prophet, so discerning and full of revelation, have you noticed that she doesn't have any children?"

And Elisha says, "Really? Now that you mention it, I guess not."

Immediately and instantly the need that she has is brought before God. Now, He knows our needs. What He is trying to

124

say to us is this: "I want to turn this thing around. And the way that I want to do it is to get you to take the focus off your needs and focus on My glory."

Think about it. You know that this woman had wept many, many days in her life over her barrenness. It was a great shame; in fact, it was considered a curse in Israel. Not only did her husband have legal right to divorce her, but she had no future security. If she outlived her husband, all of their property would go to the king and she would live at the mercy of the elders. But when she had the opportunity to point out her desperate situation, she said nothing. "I am content. All is well." That is the awesome heart of a servant. Contentment connected with the eternal promises of God. Prophecy announced miracle. And because of it, power and authority were released from the heavenlies.

God said, "You made a place for Me, and I filled it. Now I will fill that empty place in you. This time next year you will embrace a son." Outrageous!

That is why her response seems understandable. "Don't lie to me!" She had yielded her expectations. She had completely laid down the idea of a child. She was in her middle life and had resigned, consigned, come to peace with the likelihood that she would not produce an heir. Even in her barren state the Shunammite's confession was "All is well." She had filled the void with contentment in God. And godliness with contentment is great gain. She had settled all of her storms. That is why she was able to provide a place where her guests were completely at rest.

Contentment

In the past few decades there has been a progression from the "word of faith" type of prayer (known generally as "name it and claim it") into formulaic prayer (such as "here are seven steps to success"). These contemporary messages suggest that the Good News ends for us here and now in our circumstances. This has subverted the eschatological hope and message of the Gospel—the truth that Christians are firmly rooted in eternity and that their rewards are being stored up in heaven. A further problem is that even if we get more and more "stuff" and move from great position to even greater position, we never really know when we have reached the fulfillment of our goals because there is always something more to want.

The problem is one of contentment. Without it we will always be looking for more. Now obviously we have needs, and it is not wrong to pray about them. But if we get into a frenzy about what we want, it is possible to lose what we have. And, in fact, if room has not been made for the Presence to come and rest, then the opposite will come in—the spirit of restlessness.

Restlessness is rampant in our culture, and it is one of the main ways of providing an open door for the demonic. A false spirit will quickly start speaking to people who are not content. We see a great deal of this in the so-called prophetic movement today. People flit from one thing to the next, one place to the next, one revelation to the next. They are never satisfied. They need several dreams and prophetic words per week to keep them going. That is nothing more than a cycle of addiction that is feeding a religious spirit. It may be religious, it may be spiritual, but it is not the actual anointing Presence of the Holy Spirit. He will descend, but He will abide only for a moment and then leave.

The Bible likens a person with this restless spirit to a broken-down city, and if one's walls are broken down, the demonic will find places to enter and roost. The priority in this situation is not to get so many supernatural revelations per hour, but to build up the walls of the personality with basic things like daily devotions, prayer, the sacraments and Scripture. Then when a true prophetic word comes, it is so powerful it changes lives.

When we face trials, we can either put God to the test in the wrong way by our demands or suffer the difficulty with peace, settle into contentment and see the visitation of the Lord. Remember how the angels came and ministered to Jesus? Instead of using His own strength to turn the stones into bread, He waited and let His flesh be crucified. In the end God gave Him all power and authority. The ideas of testing and healing go together, in fact. When Jesus said, "You shall not tempt the Lord your God," He was anticipating Jehovah Rapha, "God Is Healer," and Jehovah Jirah, "God Is Provider." So when the devil was goading Him to give in to the discomfort of His circumstances, He was content because He was hungry only for the things of God. When Jesus quoted Scripture back to the Adversary, He was saying essentially, "All is well."

Healing from the Inside Out

I, Mahesh, had the strangest medical experience several years ago when I had emergency surgery for diverticulitis in England. They cut me open and then sort of put me together but did not sew me back up. They just put on a dressing. Why? Because they wanted the healing to come from the inside out. They knew what they were doing because when I got healed, it was a strong healing.

This is a picture of how the Lord helps us through pain and suffering into that place of contentment where He can come and abide—He heals us from the inside out. If we try to stuff things down and seal them off, they will fester. That is why we see compulsive anger, bad temper, gossip, strife, evil speaking, depression—a wound has not been healed inside and it is festering. We need to face the wounds just as soon as we can—recognize the true feelings around them, admit them to God and let Jesus come and cleanse them.

It is the blood of the Lamb. It is Calvary. That is how the wounds are healed. Jesus is the one who does it. When He stood up and identified His ministry (see Luke 4) He said, "The Spirit of the Lord is upon Me anointing Me to bring healing," and among the things He was sent to heal was the broken heart. Sometimes the need for this kind of healing is much greater than we realize. Psalm 109:22 says, "For I am poor and needy, and my heart is wounded within me." Psalm 34:18 says, "The LORD is near to those who have a broken heart." So many of us are walking around like veterans who have been in wars but the wounds are still there, especially in our hearts.

This makes it difficult to love God or ourselves or others. We may want to reach out, but if we carry unhealed hurt inside, we do not feel love. We feel worthless. How can we go tell others that the Lord loves them when we do not feel it ourselves?

For God, relationship with us remains the priority even over the manifestation of the promise. Now why is that? Because this life is temporary; He is molding us now in the same way that He picked up a handful of mud in the beginning and made man, *adam*, and breathed into him the breath of life. The Lord is making us into sons and daughters who will reign and rule with Him forever. We will be handed the eternal riches of the Kingdom of God, and we will sit with Christ to reign and rule.

God is after something that is of higher priority than the promise, and that is the vessel, the character, the formation of the mind, will and emotions, the heart, the spirit of the one to whom He has given the promise. Sometimes the promise can tarry and tarry and tarry, and you think, *God, You promised this forty years ago.* And He says, *Yes, and you're still jealous—every time you see Joe Bob with his new truck, you think* I'm still driving this old beat-up Chevy. *That cannot remain in there. That is what got Lucifer into trouble.*

And likewise, on our end, working toward becoming one with the Lord always has to remain the priority over the manifestation of the thing He promised to give us. If we get our priorities straight, a lot of times it takes a lot less time to get the manifestation of the promise.

Carrying the Hurt

When our daughter Anna was working on a paper for her master's degree in social studies, she needed to do some research on different aspects of her family roots. She called us one day with some questions about our family history.

I, Mahesh, don't usually talk about my family history much, but she needed some information so I told her various things. She knew that I was the seventh of eight children and that my parents were from India but settled in Kenya, where I was born.

My father died when my little sister and I were very small. My brother—he was about eighteen years old when I was five—took over much of the responsibility for the family. He never married; he looked after my mom and all of us and was very much like a father to me.

Well, Anna and I started talking about what happened to each of my siblings, and it brought something to mind that was very painful for me. That brother died a few years ago from cancer. He had never really asked for anything in all those years of serving the family, but before he passed away, when he was fading, he made one request—of me.

129

Bonnie and I had been planning key outreaches and evangelistic meetings with a group of pastors in Taiwan for over a year. I was due to go to Taiwan in just a few days, when we learned that my brother was growing weaker. My heart was torn between my desire to go to my brother and the burden the Lord had given me for this outreach. I also realized that if I cancelled, the Chinese pastors would lose face among their people. The servant of God who was to lead their advertised campaigns would not be there and would bring humiliation to them.

We prayed and asked the Lord for direction. I remember we specifically prayed that we would hear from my brother before I left if we were to cancel the trip. The next few days passed with no news from my family. Then, literally hours into my flight to Taiwan Bonnie got the call.

My brother, who was in England, had taken a turn for the worse. He had just one request: He wanted to see me before he passed away. Bonnie called me as soon as I landed in Taiwan. We knew from the timing of the call that it was God's answer. It was one of the most painful times in my life, but I let the answer from God determine my decision rather than my very real feelings of love and desire to honor and be with my brother in his last hours on this earth. Because I committed myself to be with those pastors, hundreds were getting saved in cities that would normally see maybe one or two salvations a month. I was watching this miracle work of God in the services and outreaches—and yet my brother had said, "I just want to see you." I had committed myself to do the Lord's work—and yet my brother was calling me.

I had to make the decision to obey the Lord and not do that one thing for the person who had given everything for me. I did not get to see him. And it hurt. It was not anything bad that I had done, but I felt that I had failed my brother. He lived honorably before me all his life; I failed him. And I carried that deep hurt for a very long time.

One day some time after that, I was conducting a meeting in south Florida. I was praying for people, and suddenly I felt Jesus walk into the room and stand by my side. And then He said something to me. He said, *By the way, Mahesh, because you could not go see your brother, I went in your place.* It was a word that came from the Presence of the throne. When God speaks one little word, it will totally transform you because it has such explosive power. What it said to me was that Jesus went and took my brother's hand and took him home. I did not have to be worried. And, honestly, if Jesus had given me a choice, would I rather be there or have Jesus be there? Given a choice I would rather that Jesus be there.

That word brought healing into my soul and my broken heart. It totally transformed the hurt that I had carried. Jesus did not choose on that occasion for my brother to be healed; it was time for him to go home, but without that word from the Lord, I would have carried a deep, unhealed wound. Instead I felt as though Jesus said, "You chose rightly."

So many of the choices we have to make are not easy, and they can lead to sickness in our souls. We carry these deep wounds inside in the form of hurtful memories or weak or wounded emotions. Often we find that when we pray for people they are not even able to recall the root of their pain or their hurt, or sometimes the wound is so deep they are not able to speak of it.

If we fail to take care of it, if we never allow Jesus' visitation in there or His word to come, we will find that the effect of it is to walk around with depression or a sense of worthlessness or

131

inferiority. Sometimes it causes fears that have no reason, anxieties for which there is no understanding. Even physical illness can be caused by the hurt that is in the soul. Unless Jesus touches that hurt, it will stay lodged in the memory or emotions.

Sometimes, by the way, wounds can have their source in ungodly acts that occurred generations ago that are affecting your bloodline. Those curses need to be broken—and that is just one of many reasons that Christians ought to run to take Communion. We should be grateful that we believe in the living blessing of the elements of Communion because the blood of Jesus Christ has the power to break even the hurt that is in your bloodline.

Jesus is able to heal the wounds from the inside out, and then not only heal but also fill those vacuum areas with His love. Always remember when dark things are removed to fill that space with the Presence and the love of Jesus Christ.

When Life Happens

Psalm 139:1 says, "O LORD, You have searched me and known me." First John 3:20 says, "God is greater than our heart, and knows all things." When we say that Jesus comes and heals that hurt, we are not saying that the past is changed. The past has passed. My brother went on home to be with the Lord before I could go to him. But the Lord wants to touch us in such a way that changes our response to the past and heals the pain. And then according to Romans 8:28, we know that all things work together for good. In that context, then, we release the past into God's hands and ask Him to use it for good in the present and in the future.

For all of us, life happens. We live in a fallen world. Accidents happen. Natural disasters happen. Sometimes we are hurt because people deliberately do things to wound us. Other times people hurt us and have no idea they are causing us pain. Sometimes it is because of mistakes that we ourselves make, our wrong actions, wrong responses. Some of our hurts go way back. Some are recent. See, the devil does not play fair. He comes when we are the most vulnerable. But when you welcome the glory, you can leave things there—concerns about your children, prayers about your marriage or your business. The glory will do above and beyond anything that you can pray for.

This is not just for a few people; God wants all of us to come into that realm. In fact, we do not even need a great store of faith; we just need to welcome the One who wants that kind of relationship with us.

I remember a meeting in Chicago several years ago in which six men walked up with a stretcher and, without saying a word, slipped it onto the large wooden stage where I was speaking.

My eyes fell on the stretcher and the skeletal form it carried. For a moment I thought it was a dead body, but then I realized it was a living human being—although barely living. His body was wracked with cancer, and not only was he terminally ill, but he was terminal as in a few hours or maybe minutes from death. In fact, I found out later that his pastor had already arranged his funeral. But his friends had heard that a healing evangelist was in town, and they said, "Let's go." I think they might have smuggled him out of the hospital to bring him to the meeting.

Now I have to confess that on the inside I was slightly irritated! I went straight from the glory realm to my carnal mind as I sat there looking down on that dying body and thinking, *Why did they bring this man up here? He is going to die in the next few minutes! Why didn't they ask me before they did this?* I was such a man of faith in that moment that I was worried he was going to die before my meeting was over! It is never good to have someone die when you are doing a healing service.

I went back to my message and then began to minister to some of the people in the crowd. Suddenly I noticed that there was a golden cloud all around the dying man's body. I just watched as golden waves of light and rainbow colors hovered over his form. I did not know what was happening, but I knew that the glory was there.

The next year I was back in Chicago ministering at a large church. One of the "catchers" was a tall, handsome Italian gentleman with dark hair. Wherever I went I noticed he was right there to help catch those who were slain in the Spirit. Near the end of the meeting the pastor said, "Brother Mahesh, do you remember this man?"

I said, "No, I've never met him."

"This is Tony," he said. "He is the man who came to your meeting on a stretcher last year. I had already arranged his funeral when he got healed in your service!"

God had healed him from the top of his head to the tip of his toes. It had very little to do with me. When I first saw Tony I did not immediately exercise faith. But he and his friends had gotten into the realm of the Presence of the Lord where nothing is impossible. Because of the blood of Jesus, they became carriers of the glory.

The Presence and glory of the Lord changes everything. Second Corinthians 3:18 says, "We all, with unveiled face, beholding as in a mirror the glory of the Lord, are being transformed into the same image from glory to glory, just as by the Spirit of the Lord." God wants to impart His glory into each of us, transforming us, healing us, delivering us and restoring us. The key is His Presence. The more we recognize and honor His Presence, the more we will behold His glory and the more we will begin to reflect that glory in the earthly realm.

Arise, shine, for your light has come, the Word says. The glory of the Lord is risen upon you. Jesus said to the sisters of Lazarus, "If you believe, you will see the glory of God." And the glory of God then raised a person who had been dead for four days. That is the glory.

Today is the day of salvation. It is a day of restoration, of wholeness, of healing. As Jesus comes, He heals not just our bodies but our hearts and souls as well. When we give ourselves to the anointing and welcome the Lord of glory, He calls us to that room of miracles and speaks a word that heals deep wounds, breaks curses and transforms us in the process. The Shunammite received her promise, and in the process she was healed from the inside out.

7

WHEN GOD'S PROMISES SEEM BROKEN

Then Jesus told his disciples a parable to show
them that they should always pray and not
give up.

Luke 18:1, NIV

The Shunammite Speaks . . .

Five years of grace. Each moment was like a draught of living water as I drank in the wonder of that child, my promised one with dates for eyes and hands and feet that appeared replications of his father's. At times I thought I saw his grandfather in him. And I forgot myself because I had him to care for.

It was the time of cutting the firstfruits. I watched from the rooftop as Habakkuk went into our rich harvest with his father. Our firstborn beside him, Joktan would cut the select fruit of our fields, and the harvesters would begin their work.

The crops were as bountiful as we had ever seen them, producing the best of every fruit. There would be barley and wheat in abundance both for our own provision and to sell at the market. I did not doubt that some of it would make its way by ship down to Egypt. It was the day after Shabbat of the feast of unleavened bread, and as if in tribute the heavy heads of grain ripened quickly in the hot sun.

I had noticed wisps of clouds building from the west; rainfall this time of year would be an occurrence both unseasonable and unexpected. A movement caught my eye. I saw a field hand laboring upon the path through the fields toward our house. The scene before me stole the air from my body. I gasped.

"Habakkuk!"

Down the stairs and out of our gate I flew. The slumped heads of the standing grain beat against my knees. Fear washed through me as I reached our servant. Habakkuk was burning with fever.

"He complained of his head," the servant explained. "Master ordered him home to you."

"Help me get him to the house," I said.

Taking my child on my lap, I gently bathed his face and neck with a cloth dipped in cool water. His curly dark hair, wet from his own sweat and the water I poured, curled around my fingertips like clinging vines.

After a few minutes, Habakkuk's eyes fluttered open. He weakly clutched my hand and squeezed his eyes shut in pain, his face a grimace. A tremor ran down his torso and my own body reacted with trembling. I am sure I comforted him, but with what words who could remember now? He certainly did not hear them.

I continued bathing him with the cool water. The locusts sang in the heat beyond the wall. Their trills sounded to me like an army of Levite priests standing line by line and blaring tiny shofars. I lifted my voice in a lullaby to drown out the mournful droning.

I stayed with him on my lap until noon.

Habakkuk became less and less animated. His breathing grew faint. My tension rose as one after the other of the servants would peer into the dimness with wide, wondering eyes.

One maid came to tell me that Joktan had called for food and drink to be delivered to his men in the field. The clouds were growing darker, and he could not take a chance that it would not rain. A wet crop could easily mildew, and much of the wheat would be lost.

140

My husband had asked men of our city to come and help cut and sheaf the wheat, and they would likely be working by lamplight through the night to bring the harvest into our barns.

I would not tell him what I feared. In hope against hope perhaps the boy would awaken. I placed two fingers on his hot neck. His pulse felt weaker still. My eyes filled with fearful waters, but I subdued them and gave out orders for portions to be prepared for the laborers in the harvest. The servants passed about me opening clay vessels, pouring out oil and weighing out olives and dried fruits. A stack of freshly made flatbread was wrapped in a clean cloth. In short order my little band of serving maids was sent away into our fields with food and drink for the men.

In this, the year of our greatest harvest, the most frightful specter loomed. It raged against all the goodness that had overtaken us, all the hopes that had been fulfilled. And I was impotent to intervene. I could not protect the hearth I had watched over so faithfully. My arm was too short to save my son. I sat with his listless body, useless to do anything but pour water over his head and reassure him of my love. And in the midst of my quiet murmuring, Habakkuk slipped away.

I had been afraid to move him much, but now I sat up rigid and laid both hands upon his shoulders. His head lolled to one side, and I shook him as if I could wake him. "Do you hear me? Son! Son!"

I shut my eyes against his face and prayed with all my might that he would suddenly inhale and breathe in life.

I opened them in disbelief. My world and all its courses stopped.

Was this the end of all of it? Had God's promise been fulfilled? Was this—this horrid half measure of my joy—the end of it?

Something inside of me refused to let that question go unanswered.

This cannot be! It should not be!

It shall not be.

I gathered the boy up and rose from where I had sat holding him these past hours. Clutching him tightly, I felt that he had no weight at all. I refused to accept that his breath no longer came forth from his lips. Up I went. Each step I took laid weight upon the strength of my resolve. I had built these stairs to make the way for the man of God to come to the room we made for him. He had trodden those stairs with frequency, and every day he made his abode with us our house was filled with peace. At the top of these stairs the prophet's chamber lay. On the threshold of its door the word of promise had come to me. Those words had given my son his very name: embrace.

I was glad everyone was in the fields. Under the cover of distraction with the harvest I could keep the servants' attention, as well as Joktan's, elsewhere. I feared they would restrain me if they knew. They would say the grief was too much. They would call Joktan in from the field, and he would command me to my bed, and they would take him. Take Habakkuk and lay him in the grave.

I would have none of that. I made my plan as I ascended the stairs. I would speak to no one in my household, for to speak of it seemed to agree with death and give it permission to keep its hold upon my son. I would drive it out. He would drive it out—the man of God from whose lips Habakkuk's name had first come forth.

I entered Elisha's room. It was just as he had left it. Its peace came out to meet me as though it did not notice Habakkuk's motionless form. I passed over the threshold of promise and went straight to the bed where the man of God had lain that day he spoke. There I gently laid my Habakkuk. This was the bed from which the prophet had spoken forth God's word of promise. It was from here the word of life had leapt toward my barren womb. The word of God had given him to us. The word of God that, when all the kingdoms of this world have failed, would have its way.

I looked upon the sleeping countenance of my son.

"Rest, love," I told him quietly. "Mother shall soon come back to you here."

I went out and shut the door. My hand trembled on the latch as I turned the key in the lock of the room we had built upon our roof. I held back my tears and clamped the tip of my tongue between my teeth until I thought I might bring blood. I slipped the key into my pocket, and the weight of that small bit of cast iron seemed more than the weight of the whole world. But my mind was quick with planning. I would go to the mountain of God as Abraham had done. I would see Him, Jehovah, the Lord who makes provision. Surely as there had been for my forbearer there would be for me a ram caught in the thicket of my prayers. I would go and come back again and bring back with me my living son!

I slipped quietly down the two flights of our stairs. Coming to the landing, I saw that our houseboy sat just beyond the porch of our courtyard.

"Izzak," I called him. The boy looked up.

143

"Yes, ma'am?"

"Go to your master in the field at once. Tell him your mistress has need of one of the servants and a donkey. Quickly," I urged the boy to the door and set him off. "Go now!"

Izzak ran toward the gate and disappeared beyond the wall.

The sky was ominous. Wind whipped dry leaves across the courtyard, and they tumbled with scraping sounds across the threshold of our door.

It seemed an eternity that I waited. I paced the floor and prayed under my breath all the while. And as I walked up and down, back and forth in my house, the scenes of Abraham the father of our faith continued to spin around me. Like a web of comfort they seemed to shield me from fear.

By the time my husband sent the servant and a donkey back to me I was standing impatiently in the open courtyard, saddle in hand. I know the man must have been startled to find me, the mistress of this great house, ready like a barn boy with the donkey's tack.

"Here I am, mistress," he approached me with a questioning look, leading a donkey. "Forgive me, my lady, but our master begs to know if there is something urgent." The man turned about indicating the harvest field. "The harvest—"

I had no patience for questions. I thrust the saddle toward him. "Saddle the donkey," I barked. Then I turned to address the houseboy.

"Izzak!"

He stumbled forward stuttering, "M-my lady?"

"Return to your master," I recovered for a moment and took the boy kindly by his shoulders. "Tell him your mistress sends this message: 'All is well.'"

"Yes, ma'am." He hurried away.

In another moment Joktan himself strode through the gate, the out of breath houseboy at his heels.

"What is this, wife?" Joktan exclaimed as he crossed our courtyard. The dust of harvest covered him, and his shirtsleeves were wet with sweat.

"I am going quickly to the man of God," I told him, nodding to the servant to mount.

"By heaven, wife. Why would you go today?"

"Peace, Joktan. All is well." I put my foot into the stirrup and swung myself up behind the servant. "I will return." I nudged the donkey on with my heels, and the servant obligingly guided him on.

Joktan looked stunned as we passed out of the courtyard. I avoided even a second glance in his direction. The only thoughts I would entertain were those of Abraham and his words to the servant as he went into the mountain, "The lad and I will go yonder and worship and will come back to you again."

I fingered the key tucked within the folds of my dress and closed my eyes against the dust that whipped into our eyes from the darkening skies as we turned onto the open road. On we rode, soon passing the fields where the threshing had begun, the harvesters bobbing like storks. I clung to the servant's back as the donkey carried us speedily away to the mountain marking Carmel in the distance. There I knew I would find the man of God.

And We Listen . . .

It might not seem possible, but it is often true: Things that are spoken in the glory and fulfilled in the glory will be tested. Sometimes the very thing that God gave you could be dying or dead and you think, *Why? What happened?* We saw in chapter 2 that the temptation in times of loss is to think, *It must be my fault.* This happens with dreams we hold in our hearts, and it happens when we have actually held the promise in our hands and then lost it: *What did I do wrong? I must have handled this badly.*

If things that you have received from God have been attacked, you did not suddenly drop out of the will of God. Your setback is God's setup for "miracles plus!" In other words, when something dies it is not the time to give up. The battle is just beginning.

This woman's baby, who was given through an anointed word, was attacked, in our estimation, by the devil. The child cried out, "My head, my head!" And he died. Was this the end? No, it was just the beginning! God was about to pull out His sword and do battle on her behalf. We might think that a dead womb bringing forth a child was miracle enough, but God was going to do something even greater. She did not get just one miracle; she got the impossible miracle. And you can, too.

Have you made a place for the Lord to rest? Where the glory was, it will come again. The Shunammite's story is emblematic of this. The enemy, the ultimate enemy, death, came and knocked on her door, but she was not fazed. God had given her a gift, a miracle provision, and she was not about to let it be stolen. She handled it in the most wonderful, amazing way. She had experienced God's power. She expected, therefore, that the same God of miracles would reveal Himself and defend the gift He had given her.

Her spirit, her example, her story inspire us today in every circumstance of life, wherever we are. When something troubling knocks on our doors, whether it is financial need, an infirmity or even death itself, believers should not be fazed. We are able to use that challenge as a vehicle to go from glory to glory, or into the sphere of faith beyond faith.

Here are several keys that we have found to open the way from faith to faith, from grace to grace and from glory to glory—when God's promises seem broken.

Keep Your Focus on God

Often people let go at the point of testing. They reach a place in the battle where they say, "Well, God never intended to give it to me," and they lose the fight by just leaving it alone. Maybe it is a ministry or a business. Maybe it is a relationship or a healing.

We must expect a contest for our faith. We may go through stringent testing, but the Bible says that when God blesses, He blesses with no sorrow added. The things He touches have His life in them. Life that conquers death. Remember that the consummate end of our salvation is resurrection from the dead.

The Shunammite understood this. After she had five wonderful years with this amazing miracle blessing, suddenly one day he died in her lap. He was fine in the morning. He went out to be with his dad in the field. But he got a terrible headache, and by noon he was dead. Look at this woman's response. She took the child whom God had given her into the room that she had provided and waited for God to raise him. She closed that door and went out. She went up to the mountain of the Lord.

147

We read an interesting report in a medical publication by a specialist in the field of malaria. He mentioned the story of the Shunammite's son and suggested that the child likely contracted cerebral malaria, which strikes and kills quickly.

I, Mahesh, was ministering in the Congo once and had forgotten to take the anti-malaria pill. I contracted cerebral malaria, and I never want to have that pain in my head ever again. It is pain that is deep and constant, and the misery is terrible. You are in pain so much that you want to die, and it goes on and on. In my case it went on for hours and hours. We told our prayer teams based here at home about it. They prayed for me and I was healed overnight. So I sort of have a feeling of what the Shunammite's boy was going through.

There is a verse in the Bible that is often misunderstood about our battle with the enemy. Actually, the punctuation in the King James Version of this verse suggests a meaning that later versions seem to rectify. Here is the familiar King James translation of Isaiah 59:19: "So shall they fear the name of the LORD from the west, and his glory from the rising of the sun. When the enemy shall come in like a flood, the Spirit of the LORD shall lift up a standard against him."

Later translations look at this picture from a different angle. Here are two examples.

> From the west, men will fear the name of the LORD, and from the rising of the sun, they will revere his glory. For he will come like a pent-up flood that the breath of the LORD drives along.
>
> NIV

> So they will fear the name of the LORD from the west and His glory from the rising of the sun, for He will come like a rushing stream which the wind of the LORD drives.
>
> NASB

here

We have observed that God often allows evil to mature like fruit ripening on a tree. During that process, circumstances for the righteous may become very difficult and even disheartening. However, it is the glory of those who know their God not to despair but to continue expecting His appearance—when light will triumph over darkness—just as the children of Israel waited four hundred years for their deliverance from slavery in Egypt. As John said of Jesus in his gospel, "the light shines in the darkness, and the darkness does not overwhelm it" (see John 1:5). Just when it may appear all hope is gone and there is no possibility for good to bring a turn-around, the glory of the Lord appears. This Scripture says in a word what we all must realize. In the final analysis, God will Himself defend His word, His people and His mission. And, in the fullness of time, He will come down and push back the presence and power of the enemy in order to redeem His covenant people and make a way for them. As Moses saw when He parted the sea, or as David experienced Him at Baal Perazim, He is the God who breaks through like a flood.

Set the Atmosphere for Miracles

The Shunammite believed that all was well. This was based not on her feelings, but on the never-changing, eternal Source of her peace. This belief allowed her to set the atmosphere for a miracle.

Another way to put this is to say she held her peace. She avoided the temptation to accuse God of evil. In the place of contentment all those years she had learned the discipline of keeping her mouth shut and keeping her tongue under control. The tongue, as James tells us, is like a rudder that will steer us toward different situations depending on how we use it. Often people fail to loose the atmosphere of resurrection glory because they are talking too much and complaining and allowing self-pity to consume them. Hold your peace.

If you cannot move positively, it is better to be in neutral than to be negative. If you do not know what to say, say nothing. We need to learn to discipline ourselves so that at the very least we are not doing more harm than good. We should not let the atmosphere be determined by our circumstances, or the atmosphere will soon be filled with fear or panic or other soulish emotions.

If that happens, we will revert to the strength of the flesh and we will lose the miracle. If the Shunammite had voiced soulish emotion, then her culture would have moved in and driven the scenario in an entirely different direction. The mourners would have come, and the household and community would have swept her into the belief that "The child is dead. Bury the child." She took charge of the situation. She did not let others define the terms in her time of challenge. She went and laid him on the bed of the man of God and shut the door upon him and went out. Where the glory had been, she had full expectation that the glory would come again. She was fully expecting resurrection.

Now we have every right to feel a wide range of emotions during these times of trial. But it comes down to two choices: living in the circumstances or living in faith and anointing connected to the divine Presence. Miracles come out of the realm of anointing, the invisible realm, the realm in which faith is the substance, the evidence. The Spirit of God was dwelling in her house and had done something in her body. From her service and worship, she made a place for the anointing, and the promise came. She had embraced the promise. That anointing helped her go on to pursue resurrection glory.

150

Don't Get Off Your Donkey

The Shunammite gave this word to the servant who brought the donkey: "Go! And don't slack unless I tell you to."

What about you? Has God assured you that a loved one will be healed? Has He led you to form a new business? Has He given you the first indications that your wildly dysfunctional family will be restored to wholeness? Has He shown you how to move in a new area of ministry? Then don't be jarred by the bumpy ride. Don't be discouraged that you need to detour past a watering hole now and then. Don't worry if your pace slackens when you are climbing that mountain. Stay on the donkey. If you have sight of the goal, circumstances should not compel you to turn back.

We are used to instant this and instant that. Microwaves for cooking. Jets for flying. A one-hour TV program needs to have all its loose ends neatly tied up in the time allotted. It takes maturity to hold the course—and possibly an ironclad posterior when you consider the Shunammite jostled along for sixteen miles on a trotting donkey! But don't stop now. Keep riding. Get to the One whose Temple mount is established as chief of the mountains (see Isaiah 2:2). We see Jesus as He set His face like a flint to go up to Jerusalem. We draw from His determined strength and the victory He wrought for us on the mount of Calvary. With Him as our example we set out toward and conquer our miracle mountain.

Remember, in this vein, that little acts of faith release the miracles of God. You might want to picture yourself, wherever you are, riding along with the Shunammite on her donkey. It does not hurt to say to yourself: "I'm getting on my donkey to get my miracle."

It is also helpful to have someone to agree with you, someone who is along with you for the ride, as the servant was for her.

In other words, a prayer partner, someone to agree with you, someone who believes with you, someone who understands the vision, someone who carries the same vibration from the glory. Perhaps an elder or pastor can encourage you with wisdom, guidance or counsel. The Shunammite's servant would have known how to handle the donkey.

Realize That This Is a Journey

If you have spent much time on this journey, making room for the glory and the anointing of God, you are learning to possess your relationship with God as priority. And you are also likely to see that God has you in the process of an ongoing redemptive work.

Often the most important leg of the journey begins when we've come to the end of ourselves. Do you remember Jonah?

We have our own theory about why the Ninevites decide to listen to Jonah. It is probably not so much the anointing on the man of God as the fact that he has been processing in the saliva juices of a fish for three full days.

Jonah does not want to be a minister of mercy and grace to the people God is sending him to. He wants them all to die. He wants to call down fire from heaven. But God has something else in mind. So Jonah gets a ticket on a ship going in one direction, and God sends a storm and a fish to take him in the other direction.

It is when he is in the belly of the fish that Jonah gets his great visitation of God. All of a sudden, he is God's man of faith and power, ready to do His will. But at that particular moment he is in the belly of a great fish with seaweed wrapped around his head. Can you imagine what it smelled like in there? People have actually done experiments with fish saliva and have determined that the first thing to go would be his clothes. Then his hair. Then the first few layers of skin would begin to dissolve. That is the state he is in when, by about the third day, the fish vomits him onto shore.

So now here is this naked, hairless, leprous-looking man of God lying in a pool of fish vomit on a sandy seashore. Imagine him walking to town! Have you ever noticed that God kept him in the belly of that fish for as many days as it was going to take him to cross the city with the message? It keeps him moving forward: He does not want to go near the sea!

Thus, when Jonah walks into Nineveh saying, "I have a message for you from God," people are amazed. They say, "We had better listen or that's going to happen to us!"

Or think of the process for Abraham, who tries to manifest the promise with Sarah's maid and winds up with a thirteen-year-old-oops!-work-of-the-flesh to deal with and *still* does not possess the promise. But he has heard the voice of God calling him, saying, "I am God, Shaddai, Almighty, the God of the mountain. Walk in My Presence and be wholehearted." He receives the promise, and when God calls him to journey with that son of promise up the mountain and sacrifice him on the altar, Abraham can comply because he knows God will resurrect the promise to life.

Wrestle It Through

We could follow this principle of God's delight to fulfill His promises in His people further throughout the Bible—Job, Hannah, Joseph, Jacob, Anna. God looked for earthen vessels who were willing to follow Him with wholehearted commitment even when it looked as though His promise could not come true.

Their response to His promise—and our response—produces a covenant with conditions that both parties must honor. God's part is unbreakable and unbroken, but our part tends to waver with the challenges of wrestling against principalities, powers, spiritual forces of wickedness in high places as well as dealing with our own flesh. Yet if we are faithful to gird up our loins and wrestle for the blessing, we will see things that the fathers of our faith hoped for, lived and died for. Jesus Himself wrestled through the days of His journey on this earth that we might have the promise of the Father, His Holy Spirit, and do greater works than He did. The Shunammite became the steward of a gift. When the gift was taken away she went to the Source in search of its life. In Him she was confident that "all is well." In His Presence she found the consolation she sought.

Like the Shunammite, we are stewarding something. We are containers of the last-day miracles of God—salvations, deliverances, healings. In her case it was a son. In your case it may be a dead marriage, a dead business, a dead ministry. Whatever it is, put it on that bed where the double portion has slept. Then go forward, never slacking until you get your answer. Will you face hindrances? Yes. But if you are alive and if you are full of hope and if you have been anointed, you, like the Shunammite, can expect the "miracle plus."

8

RESURRECTION DAY

But Christ has indeed been raised from the
dead, the firstfruits of those who have fallen
asleep.

1 Corinthians 15:20, NIV

The Shunammite Speaks . . .

As the donkey gradually slowed under her burden, the servant began walking alongside, keeping pace. For more than a half-day's journey I had ridden, and with every jounce another word of intercession left my lips. I had hardly taken my eyes off the mountain. That peak became for me Sinai, and the man of God, Moses. The ancients tell us that God had wrapped Himself in His *tallit* and come down to meet with Moses. When the deliverer descended that mountain, the reflected glory still shone on his face. Would my face shine today? Would God come down to me? Would I see His glory?

At last, the sun having traveled a good portion of the sky, we were making our way through the wild rockrose and thorny broom that had turned the hillside pink and white and yellow. The final stretch of our journey led through calliprinos oaks, which crouched like so many dusty green beasts conferring with one another up and down the incline and out onto the plain where their acorns had blown in past seasons.

I saw a figure coming down the path to meet us. It was Gehazi. That day I thought he had the face of an angel, for his appearance meant that the prophet was here. Gehazi reached us and expressed his master's concern for me and my husband and the boy.

"All is well," I said and strained to look farther up the path.

Clutching the horn of the saddle, my dress bunched in an unwomanly fashion about me, I clung to the sloping back of the animal as we ascended the final steps to the terrace of Elisha's house.

And there he stood.

I clambered out of the saddle and ran to him. Falling at his feet, I clutched Elisha's ankles, clinging to them as if clinging to the life breath of my son.

Gehazi's hands reached as if to pull me away.

"No," said the prophet. "Do not restrain her. She is in deep distress and the Lord has hidden it from me."

"Did I ask you for a son?" I finally screamed between pent-up sobs. "Did I not beg you not to deceive me? Did I not ask you not to lie?"

Then the prophet knew.

"Gehazi! Take my staff." Elisha held out the rod of wood that he had so long leaned upon. It was like Moses extending it in power over the Sea of Reeds. "Speak to no one. If anyone greets you do not even reply. Do not be detained for any reason but run now to Shunem and lay my staff on the face of the child."

Just as Gehazi tucked his garment up into his belt and clutched the staff of power with both hands, thunder rolled in from the sea. I suddenly remembered the key! I had shut up the room. I fumbled in the folds of my dress. Catching his hand, I pushed my key into his palm. He started down the mountain at a run.

Then Elisha helped me up.

"Return Shunammite," he said simply. "Go back. Return to your house now. I have sent my servant to wake the boy."

But I would have none of it. I fell down upon his feet again and wrapped my arms around his legs. The edge of that hair coat that had clothed the man of God for many seasons filled my vision.

"No, my lord!" I told him. "I shall not return. I will not leave here until you return with me!" I would stay there on that mountain for one or two or three days believing. As long as it would take, I would not relent. I would stay until he handed my son back into my bosom.

I looked up, and the clear hazel eyes of the prophet met mine. They were full of kindness and understanding. Elisha raised his face to heaven. When he looked back at me again he consented.

"Let's go down," he said.

Back over the plain we rode in silence, the prophet and I. The slowness of our journey was torturous, for the servant led the donkey at a pace that would ensure its stamina for the miles ahead.

When we came at last within view of Shunem the sun in the west was setting beneath the suspended storm. The harvesters with Joktan did not look up as we walked silently by. I could hear them singing to one another as they threshed and separated the sheaves. Their hearts were glad. God had blessed their increase and had held back the storm as well. They were intent upon their work. Soon they would light torches and continue into the night.

Gehazi was coming out to meet us. "The boy has not awakened," he told the prophet.

I turned my face away and covered it with my veil.

Elisha swung his leg up over the donkey's neck and slipped down.

"I shall go up to him alone," Elisha said.

I nodded, dismounted and followed him into the house.

I could not sit down at any chaise or settle by the hearth. Instead I stood uncomfortably like a visitor waiting to be received. The housemaids said nothing, but I imagined that by this unusual activity in the house they had guessed at the severity of the child's illness. I could tell they prayed. I did not see the scene that followed, but the whole household soon learned of it from the prophet himself.

Inside the room the lamp cast pale light over the motionless body of the boy. His face was serene, his hands folded gently one on top of the other.

Elisha went cautiously near, as if a sudden movement might disturb the child. He stood over the bed that was his own place of repose. The bed where the word of the Lord for Israel had come in dreams often. The very bed from which the promise of this boy's life had come.

Elisha touched Habakkuk's face. His heart constricted for a moment within his throat but then something else, that unseen Greater Hand on which he leaned, buoyed him. Then, like a memory of his own, the scenes of his old master came to mind. Scenes of another house and another boy who lay dead, the widow's son in Zarephath whom Elijah had raised.

The prophet leaned his staff against the bedside. A surge of potent faith raised a vigorous head within his belly. *Hear O Israel! The Lord! The Lord is One!*

Elisha moved. Up and down he strode, back and forth before the bedside. Sometimes his hands were raised in the air. Sometimes they clasped one another and wrung themselves out with the words of his inward prayer. Sometimes facing the boy and sometimes turned away, Elisha paced. But still the presence of death seemed a chasm that no man could leap across—at least not cross and come back again. In himself he knew he could not make that leap to bring the boy's spirit back. The gulf was too wide.

But God is not a man that He should lie!
The prophet paced across the vermilion carpet and prayed again. His eyes closed as he turned from wall to wall. Sweat drops began to form on his brow.

Lord of glory, Thou art no debtor to any man!
He closed his eyes, brows furrowed in great effort searching, seeking, flying through the realm between that room and the chambers of the highest heaven.

Let me see Your glory! prayed the man who had received a double portion of his master's anointing.

Though he stood upright, within him the great servant of God was sprawled upon his face before that throne, that judgment seat where mercy triumphs.

Suddenly he saw. The room was filled. There all around him were a thousand fluttering wings of angels and the whoosh of living creatures so terrifying that if their voices were heard the earth would suddenly be still. The God of glory Himself came near His servant.

The image of his master in his mind's eye, Elisha climbed upon the bed.

Eye to eye, hand on hand, his mouth on the very mouth of the child, the servant crouched like a lion over prey. And then Elisha breathed. It was not with force of human flesh he breathed that breath, nor with the will of human mind. He was simply a vessel, one with the glory. The small body warmed beneath the prophet's touch. Elisha felt it and backed away suddenly, watching, waiting, looking to see the boy's nostrils flare to life again. His eyes passed to Habakkuk's chest.

Did it rise and fall?

Habakkuk lay still, but there was a blush of warmth in his hands.

The first time he crouched over him Elisha had had no great feeling of power. The surge of faith that came

161

from the Presence and filled the room seemed to emanate from his belly more than from his mind.

But the intercessor had withdrawn too soon it seemed, for the boy's breath did not return. Habakkuk was suspended somewhere between this world and the next. At that realization a sense of holy indignation at the powers of darkness that refused to let the child return filled the man of God. He crouched over the body again and pressed his head against Habakkuk's head. Eye to eye, mouth to mouth again Elisha breathed. Dark rose the specter of a serpent, its head and mouth and eyes pushing back against the prophet's as if to shriek: "You shall not have him!"

But the Spirit within Elisha simply breathed, exhaling life. In that moment Elisha seemed transported somewhere outside himself as if he had moved out while God moved in. And when the closed eyes of Habakkuk suddenly popped open and the boy began to sneeze, Elisha's heart nearly burst with relief.

Habakkuk's gaze lifted as if from a dreamy fog, eyes wide and innocent. The boy seemed not to recognize the friend who hovered over him.

There were no words of prayer or any other exclamation to be made in that moment of this great wondrous act of Jehovah's supreme power. There was no reply adequate that could speak to what the prophet had witnessed. Life from the dead! The greatest miracle of all—right before his very eyes. It was unspeakable.

"Gehazi," the prophet called low. The latch of the chamber door lifted, and the servant peered in.

"My lord?" Gehazi said.

Elisha's voice cracked as the sound of it came forth. "Call the Shunammite."

And We Listen . . .

Today, what dead thing are you lying on? God has this word for you and for your family, for your hopes, for your dreams, for all of the promises that you have embraced as your own. It is, in fact, even a word for cities and nations that are dying or whose economies are wilting. *God wants to resuscitate and restore and resurrect.* Our God is a God of resurrections. He is a God of miracles, signs and wonders. If you make room for Him, you will activate the miracle glory.

This is not a science. As you have no doubt gathered throughout this book, it is an art. We do not step into miracles by chasing after them. We step into miracles by seeking with all of our hearts the One who comes with resurrection power.

We have authority in the realm of miracles only because of what Jesus has done. As we make room for Him and grow in our relationship with Him, we make that place for the miracle. The glory is there. Let's look more closely at the art of getting into His glory.

Revival of the Full Gospel

Jesus' ministry of Good News, which fulfilled all the prophetic Scriptures through the Old Testament, focused on healing and deliverance. It is very plain: The Bible says that "God anointed Jesus of Nazareth with the Holy Spirit and power, and . . . he went around doing good and healing all who were under the power of the devil, because God was with him" (Acts 10:38,

NIV). Healing and deliverance from demons are two primary manifestations of the advance of the Kingdom of light.

It is also very plain that Satan has two opposing primary goals: to dominate the world and to receive the worship that belongs to God. And so as we see darkness increasing—strife, wars, conflict—we should recognize that we are in a wonderful time of opportunity for advancing the Kingdom of light.

And, in fact, today we are seeing a revival of the full Gospel— the Gospel is being proclaimed and signs and wonders are following. Truly it is wonderful to know personally and individually how significant our lives are in this hour. Believers in the Christ are the people who are capable of praying down revival, of bringing down the glory of God. The whole world is a stage that is set up for the Church of the living God to arise and let her light shine.

How do we get this victory? We step into the victory that Christ has already won for us. Colossians 2:15 states that through the cross, Jesus disarmed the rulers and authorities and put them to open shame by triumphing over them. Jesus ransacked them. He took away all their weapons and gave that victory to the Church. In the Great Commission, when He said, "Go into all the world and preach the Gospel, and signs and wonders, miracles of healing and deliverance will follow you" (see Mark 16:15–19), He was basically saying, "Execute My victory." We already possess the victory; now it is a matter of making it manifest on the earth.

Entering into Your Miracle

As you embrace the truth of Jesus' victory, do not let go if your miracle is not readily apparent. When the Shunammite reached Elisha, she did not immediately receive the miracle she was seeking. Elisha sent Gehazi ahead with Elisha's staff and instructions to lay it across the boy's face. Sometimes God gives a token in advance of His miracle. The token is the indicator that God is on the way with the final answer. Elisha's staff was the point of contact with the glory to come. Like Aaron's rod it was symbolic of life in the anointing.

Your token may be a prophetic promise, a Scripture quickened, a dream or vision you receive. It may be a partial breakthrough. Steward the token and realize the final answer is on the way. The Shunammite welcomed the token while remaining steadfast at the feet of Elisha until she saw her promise live again. Do not disdain the tokens God gives. They connect you to the glory until the answer comes.

This is what Bonnie and I did regarding Aaron's birth, as we told in chapter 1. When she was pregnant with Aaron the Lord told her, *You will have a son. Name him Aaron for I will make the rod of his life bud as I did Aaron's rod of old.* This word came weeks before Aaron was born, at a time when there was no sign of life and Bonnie's body was in continual distress.

From that word, that token, we embraced confidence that in the glory a dead stick can become a fruit-bearing tree! The moment Aaron was born, four months premature with major complications and disease, Bonnie said, "It's a boy, isn't it?" As the doctor nodded, a look of terrible distress on his face in light of the impossible state of the tiny child in his hands, Bonnie declared, "His name is Aaron, and he will live and not die." She held on to the token that was given her before, and God honored His word.

Religion has given us the wrong perception of miracles. We have been trained to see ourselves apart from the problem, removed from the solution. But as Christians we are ambassadors of heaven. We carry the Solution Himself! Jesus is our miracle. Alive, as seen by His disciples when He was raised from the grave, He indwells us by His Spirit. Carrying the Living Christ, we can enter the problem with the Solution. As you dwell in His Presence you become one with Him—one with your miracle.

Scripture is a particularly powerful tool in this regard. God's Word is eternal. It is living, active and filled with His power to create. God reveals Himself and His glory in His Word. The more you meditate on the Word of God, the more you become congruent with Him. The Word is true at every level. The night before Aaron was born Bonnie dreamed the Lord spoke words from Psalm 29 over her. The next day those words entered her body in a living experience and brought Aaron forth from her body. She and Aaron became one with the Living Word. The Word of God vibrates with the glory of heaven. As you pick up its vibration what is happening in heaven happens where you are on earth.

Our first child, Ben, was born with terminal kidney disease. When Ben was sick and dying, I, Bonnie, remember that Mahesh took his Bible and got a notebook and wrote down every Scripture he could find on healing. That notebook recorded our inheritance in Jesus, the promises, the prophetic words. God is true to His Word. When no doctors could help us, we—and the dear ones watching with us by prayer and fasting—held on to that lifeline of the Word.

One of the first verses we claimed was Exodus 23:25: "Ye shall serve the LORD your God, and he shall bless thy bread, and thy water; and I will take sickness away from the midst of thee" (KJV). As we stood on that Scripture, we saw the glory of the Lord come around Ben in a miraculous way. The Lord healed him completely—his kidneys, his whole urinary system. Because we experienced it, we know it is true. We can possess it for those who need healing. Now when we pray for healing—particularly for children—that is one of the first verses we claim because of our own experience.

Wherever you have experienced God in the past, experience Him again. This is what the Shunammite did. God came and gave her a son. That showed her that it was His will to heal her, to bless her, to make her fruitful and productive. Then when the child died, she could go to Him and say, "God, I know who You are. I will not accept death here because You are the God of life."

See Jesus More Clearly

God is shaking our circumstances so that we can see Jesus more clearly. It is as though you are climbing the mountain of His glory. People, agents of the enemy, will try to hold on to your leg so that you stay in the low levels rather than move higher where His glory is.

Childless Hannah is a good example of this. She had a husband, Elkanah, but she also had a rival—Elkanah's other wife. That rival was the voice of the enemy in a sense. She provoked Hannah severely. She made her miserable. First Samuel 1:7–10 says that year after year, when Elkanah took his family up to the house of the Lord, her rival provoked her. Hannah's heart was so grieved she wept and did not eat. She was in great anguish.

That is what the enemy does. He comes in the midst of your need to make you miserable. The question then becomes: When you are in the middle of the need, how intensely do you want to enter into the Lord's provision? If you are serious about emerging with the miracle, this is when you make your relationship with God more intense. Some people would focus here on their battle against the enemy. The better choice is to become more intense toward the Lord, to praise and worship and welcome Him.

Jesus took His disciples up to the top of the mountain where His glory shone. It is as though they knew Him as Clark Kent, but then they saw Him as Superman! When the challenge comes, when the promise dies, do not get fearful. Do not listen to the thief, the robber, the destroyer. This is simply a setup for Jesus to become even more glorious.

See, the enemy is trying to play with your mind, to make you anxious and fretful. You need to go into the house of the Lord, into the house of prayer, into the house of glory. You will find that when you enter the heart of prayer you are setting yourself up for resurrection of the miracle.

What dead thing are you lying on? You may be the one to breathe life into a child, a dream, a ministry in an inner city. Become an agent of the miracle-working glory of God. This is the hour when cities and nations that have been considered dead are going to be revived because His agents are going to be there speaking life and glory.

We possess the victory; now it is time to make it manifest. Rise, shine, become a carrier of resurrection glory.

9

ROOM FOR MORE MIRACLES

"Eye has not seen, nor ear heard, nor have entered into the heart of man the things which God has prepared for those who love Him."

1 Corinthians 2:9

The Shunammite Speaks . . .

The flicker from the lampstand was the first thing visible as the door swung open. Then, the feet of our son standing upon the floor and just behind him, the man of God.

"Mother?"

He's alive!

Jehovah, the strength of my life, had answered! Habakkuk was alive again!

I thought my heart would burst with wild relief and joy. Tears of unspeakable gratitude flooded my eyes, and I fell down before the servant of the King of heaven.

"Blessed be the God of our fathers. Blessed be the God of Elisha who has heard my cry and answered me today!" I flung myself upon his ankles once again but this time in celebration. "Thanks be to God, my Lord, whom you serve!"

Elisha touched the top of my head slightly. "Take your son."

"I'm hungry, Mother!" Habakkuk said. I burst into laughter and gathered him into my arms.

"Shunammite?" Elisha spoke again.

"My lord?" I turned toward him.

"Famine comes," the prophet said, his countenance as if beholding a furnace blast. He looked to be a man exhausted from the visions he beheld in the wake of the resurrection.

I learned that the power that coursed from the Presence of the Lord had been at first as sweet as honey in his mouth. But it had turned to bitterness when He who holds all knowledge had passed by. In His wake as if carried in His train, there were dark clouds, dust swirling, and out of the storm Elisha heard the cries of a nation in anguish. Pestilence. Israel begging bread and languishing from lack of water.

The immediate future of our people. A recompense for sin in turning from the Lord to empty idols. God's people had filled themselves with vanity. They trusted in the strength of their own flesh to save them. The plenteous harvest had filled the fruitful land, but His people had forgotten their God. Religious and useless. Like sheep without a shepherd or a child who refuses correction. No imagination was too vain to pursue, no doctrine too perverse to proclaim.

The Lord would empty Israel's storehouses as He emptied their bellies. He would empty their pockets and turn their revelries and feasts to mourning and cleanness of teeth. He would pour out His judgments until they came to the end of themselves and returned to the God who loved them. Cleansing would come like a refiner's fire.

Elisha had watched in his vision as flames dried up the ocean and burned up the land. They licked at the prophet's garments and seemed to singe his beard and smoke the very hair of his arms. His body felt the racking pangs of hunger from a nation in famine and darkness of soul.

Gehazi stared wide-eyed.

Then as if regaining strength, Elisha looked at me directly, his gaze stern and clear.

"Rejoice today for the return of your son. Let your house and husband and the harvesters fill the barns and store up food in your larder. Give thanks and praise the Lord who gives seed to the sower and bread to the eater. Remember this harvest," Elisha said.

The red storm of blowing dust and the cries of hungry anguish had folded up as a tent and disappeared as the vision had come to him. In its wake the word of the Lord dropped down upon his servant, and Elisha spoke from a place of knowing what natural men cannot discover—the knowledge of what was to come.

"This is what the Lord says, noblewoman: 'By this time next year there shall begin seven years of severity in Israel.'"

In just an instant my thrill at seeing Habakkuk drained out of me as if from a vessel suddenly pierced. It was a strange moment. Since the day I had compelled Elisha to come to our house, the room we had built had become the place of unusual encounters. They were bitter as well as sweet. But I knew as surely as I stood there that the word from the man of God would surely come to pass.

"What shall we do?" I asked him.

"You must take your household and turn aside in the land of the Philistines until the famine is past."

"Philistia? The land of our enemies?"

There is much I could tell you of our next seven years. The Philistines were men of long smooth hair and flowing garments, who sometimes carved dark inked figures on their skin and who ate unclean food of swine and even dogs! Their wine feasts and cultic worship surpassed the sins of Israel.

173

In the first years of our sojourning Joktan employed himself at the bellows, for the Philistines used much iron work and kept an arsenal. When Joktan began to grow weak with age he took young Habakkuk along with him. Our boy came home drenched in man's sweat. And inside I would pray God forbid that any spear or arrow thus forged be used against our people.

More and more Habakkuk asked for stories of our forefathers and of our religion. He could sit for hours listening. So while we were in exile, we were not without the Presence or the blessing of Jehovah. And while we longed for home and had to keep ourselves separate for caution's sake, we were not ungrateful or without times enriched with joy.

Though Joktan was faithful and skillful the work was hard on his body. In the sixth year my husband fell ill and did not recover. His last request was that Habakkuk and I take his bones with us when we returned to our city. I gave him my word, and as my tears fell I held his hand tightly to my heart with the gratitude of a wife who has been cherished.

My maids and I continued to work with flax and weave and sell garments to the merchants. Habakkuk, a boy/man in his twelfth year, also continued at the smith's forge. We worked and watched and waited and knew that God would come and deliver us.

On a day in late summer a full year after my widowhood the news came that famine in Israel had ended.

Home! We were going home at last!

When finally we came into the valley between our mountains, Gilboa and Tabor, we were a picture of Issachar's banner when Israel of old went out from Egypt—

174

our laden donkeys going up surefooted between the mounts of blessing and cursing, and Habakkuk and I riding in the ox cart being drawn along. As I had promised, Joktan's remains came with us to be laid to rest with his fathers once we reached Shunem.

We were not prepared for the sight that met us when we crossed into the inheritance of our tribe. Seven years she had been deprived of rain and loving husbandry. The famine was ended, but the land was only beginning its recovery.

Was this my Jezreel?

She had languished severely. Her trees were crooked spines, their bones without the fatted flesh of leaf and fruit. Her terraces were full of unturned stones and scars where the plow had finally given up the blade. I felt I could see ghosts of bent figures scraping for the last dried pods or dust-laden remnants of a former harvest, scavengers slowly plodding between empty homesteads searching for something to feed their famished children.

As we ascended the outcrop I strained forward as Shunem at last came into view. The first buds of her recovery were evident. A farmer plowed a terrace in the distance. I was confused as the plots had taken different shapes. I looked toward our vineyard to see a watchman in the tower, and my heart leaped. There were workers, but whose?

I shivered in cold prophetic anticipation of the scene within our courtyard. I feared I would find our old rooms scarred and abused by vagrants.

We turned down the lane and made the last few paces carefully, the servants following my lead. This was not the joyful return I had imagined. Militia men lined the lane. At our gate our entourage came to a rumbling stop.

"Halt, there!" A king's militiaman called out sharply. "This is king's property. Whom do you seek?"

King's property!

"This is the house of Joktan, and adjoining the house of my father before him," I told the man. "I am returned after seven years' sojourn. I have brought the heir to his estate."

"Call the captain," the gate man barked behind him across my courtyard while he barred our way. "This woman claims it is her house." He told me, "You may stand inside. The others must wait here. Which one is the heir?"

Before I could answer Habakkuk spoke.

"Here! It is I," he said. In an instant he was standing straight and protective at my side.

We two stepped over the threshold into our courtyard and found it full of strangers.

Inside the gate were stabled militia horses, and men sat and stood and slept in the open space. Their arms and gear were in piles here and there. A fire smoked in the pit, and two men squatted there attending whatever it was they boiled in the pot.

Our beautiful noble house an occupation camp!

"You can bring yourselves and spend the night in the courtyard, but in the morning you will have to find new quarters," the captain said.

I was speechless. The home I had come back to was not mine to have. Habakkuk's estate stolen! Our security gone!

My pleas brought only a shrug and the advice to appeal to the king.

Once we were resettled safely within the walls of one of our tribesmen, I turned to our only recourse. And of all the sights I could never have imagined when I came home, the most astounding waited for Habakkuk and me in King Joram's court. We made our entreaty and entered the portico of his famed ivory palace. The cool of the interior was welcome compared to the open sun. The pillars like carved palms resembled a forest! Egyptian motifs adorned the walls and circled the pillar bottoms.

Influence of Queen Jezebel, I thought.

I could not imagine there had been any lack within these walls. The portico thronged with audience of every sort. There were courtiers, militiamen, a few wizened councilmen. Habakkuk and I sat down among several others who had come to beg audience for a variety of complaints. The messenger returned almost immediately to us and waved us hurriedly in, to the disfavor of some who called out that they had been waiting for two days.

Our footsteps sounded hollow as we followed the king's man along the passageway. As we ascended the stair to the second tier with the throne room itself, I prayed for courage and the right words.

We came into the king's hall at last and found that it, too, was full of people, though less crowded. I surmised these were elders from several cities, commanders of the king and some noblewomen with their husbands who had been invited to sit at the king's table. People came and went, and all seemed either to be accustomed to being there or else be engaged in some occupation. Habakkuk and I hid ourselves among them and waited to be called while the courier took my case to the scribe.

I came to realize that the people were the audience of some entertainment, as all eyes were on a wiry frame that talked and gestured. As my senses adjusted to the sights and sounds, his voice commanded my attention. It was strangely familiar. Through the onlookers I strained to see and discovered he was wrapped in a number of bandages, as lepers were. Suddenly I knew who it was.

Gehazi!

Yet, was he a leper? What was he doing in the king's presence? And where was his master?

My worst fears for Elisha's survival with this apostate king might be realized.

As my eyes adjusted to the sight, so did my ears. Gehazi was very animated and telling a story that I knew well. He was telling my own story! He described my ride across the Esdraelon and how I threw myself upon his old master's feet. Then the story became the tale of Gehazi running back to the noblewoman's house, Elisha's staff firm in his hand.

The king lounged in his chair, a smile languid on his face. I had imagined King Joram to be an imposing character and was surprised to find him rather an ordinary-looking person. But beside him sat a far less ordinary regent.

The queen of whom I had heard since my childhood was strikingly beautiful. She carried herself tall and straight as though some craftsman had shaped her figure out of porcelain and painted it with colors of Phoenicia. It was impossible to guess her age, but I knew her to be at least half again my own. Her eyes were lined in the manner of the Egyptians with kohl and dragon emerald and her attire was Phoenician; one bare shoulder was trimmed in gold that would have paid a year's hire. Her hair was neatly coifed. She seemed to float rather than sit on the chair beside her son. She wore a cold, proud look.

Jezebel, the infamous murderess!

I prayed the Shema within my heart and gripped Habakkuk's hand.

Gehazi spoke on, animating every detail, and his audience appreciated all his antics. He became the center of the drama and was fully in his element as jester of this court. One might think he had raised the boy himself.

Habakkuk sat transfixed to hear his story.

"The woman came in and took her son and flung him in the air," Gehazi was saying. The audience gasped and clapped.

"And then he told her, 'Famine comes!'"

The court mumbled words of resentment. Who among them had not suffered for seven years?

The queen was iced yet smiling still.

"Where is this noblewoman now?" Joram's voice broke the tension. "And the boy? Do they still reside there in that town—in Shunem?"

I found myself pushing through the audience in answer to his question, and before Gehazi could speak I said, "Here! Sire! I am the woman. I am the Shunammite of whom your servant speaks. This is my son who was dead and is now alive."

My blood was racing, pounding in my head.

The room broke into great excitement.

"For truth! Shunammite! Boy!" Gehazi shouted. He grinned from ear to ear beneath his bandages and I thought he would rush toward us.

The king waved his hand at two courtiers near us. In a moment they had me by both arms almost carrying me forward. Habakkuk, still holding one hand, was pulled behind.

"Bring the Shunammite here. I would see her closely and hear from her own lips. Bring her here!" Joram barked. "Is this the woman?" he asked Gehazi.

My old guest raised a hand.

"It is, my liege!" Gehazi gushed, amazed. "She of whom I was just speaking, sire! The very same noblewoman of Shunem!"

On their thrones Joram and his mother sat leaning forward staring at Habakkuk and myself.

"Approach, Shunammite," the king waved me forward. "And you, boy. Come nearer so we can see you."

My son and I were now on exhibit.

"So it was in your house this miracle of Elisha happened, was it?" Joram was saying. Leaning forward, he looked me directly in the eye.

"Yes, sire," I bowed before the throne and his court.

"So this is the woman whose son Elisha restored," Jezebel remarked. Her voice wrapped around us when she spoke, but it was more of a strangle than a comment. Her eyes drifted over me, taking in my figure and face with alarming interest. When she turned her gaze on Habakkuk I wanted to grab him and run from the court.

Habakkuk, on the other hand, seemed amused. He was watching Jezebel watch him.

There we were face to face. Two mothers and their sons. The daughter of Baal's high priest with the king of Israel. The daughter of the God of Israel with a nobleman's heir. The two seated in riches seemed to have every aspect of their lives secure. The two before them had nothing at all but their faith.

At the king's request and fighting a tremor in my voice, I told how Jehovah had worked through Elisha and wrought His miracles in my life. Every time I mentioned Elisha I saw in the corner of my eye the queen's look turn to stone. That reaction in her somehow gave me the sense that Elisha was still alive and still her enemy. I knew I would see him again. Inside I smiled and went on more boldly with our story, all the while determining how I would frame the request for which we had come.

The king questioned Habakkuk, prying for any hint of life beyond this realm and whether there was an afterward that burned with fire or torment. As if the boy would have been sentenced there!

Then Joram asked Habakkuk, "Have you anything else to tell me?"

"Yes, sire," he said. "We have come to recover our estate." I caught my breath at his assurance. He continued. "I am the rightful heir of my father's lands, sire. I would take my mother home."

I trembled with pride as he spoke. I had come to put myself at the mercy of this king in hopes he would grant my son's inheritance and my security. But Habakkuk had asked for our estate himself! What future was in store for this son of mine?

King Joram turned to the scribe who sat silently on the side of the hall copiously writing down our account throughout the interview, from time to time looking at us with some wonderment.

"A letter and my seal," Joram ordered.

The audience looked on eagerly.

Did they see me shiver slightly, waiting for the king's decree? What would be the fate of the woman and her son who had given succor to the prophet who had both begun and ended the famine Israel had suffered?

"Write!" Joram told the scribe. "To the commander of the king's militia: By order of Israel's sovereign on this day the Shunammite and her son . . ."

I was suspended. In his next words our fate would be decided for us. I was still as a stone.

Then Joram raised his hand. "Shall have their entire estate restored! Seal it in my name."

Gehazi's eyes met mine. He was as amazed as I. The providence of my appearing had put him in good standing above whatever had gotten him this audience already. And his favor here had created opportunity for my request. I bowed my head acknowledging the history Gehazi shared with me, and together we marveled at the God of Israel.

"So you were in Philistia?" the king asked me as the scribe scribbled.

"We were, sire."

"And how did you find it?"

"Not like Israel, sire. Not like Shunem."

"How long was your sojourn, Shunammite?" Joram asked.

"Seven full years," I told him.

Jezebel smiled. "How providential for you," she said quietly. Her teeth glinted smooth and white between tinted lips. "The length of the famine here."

Joram laughed.

"And your providence continues, noblewoman," he said. "I shall repay you for the use of your land and house." He called his commander to his side. "The king's treasury shall reimburse the noblewoman's estate for these seven years. And you shall order an escort to see her and her son safely back to Shunem with their goods."

Our land and houses and seven years' lease!

The audience of the court clapped and remarked at the king's generosity and righteousness. The commander bowed while I saw stars and willed my knees to stand firm. The first miracle that God had wrought for me had in turn wrought a second and now a third: the restoration of all that we had lost. The son I had embraced would embrace his inheritance. We would return to possess it with repayment from the king's treasury restoring the house and land as it had been in its finest day.

How I wished Joktan had lived to see this.

Our son spoke once more, squaring his shoulders to take up the responsibility his father had left him. "I thank you, sire," he said with a bow. He turned to the queen. "Thank you, lady."

Then he turned to me. "Mother," he said, "let's go home."

In the days that would come Elisha would hear of our return and come by Shunem. He would stay on our rooftop in the room we had made for him, the room of miracles. We would exchange our tales of all that had occurred. Elisha would watch Habakkuk grow and one day bless his marriage, and I would see my grandchildren.

Within the year King Joram would meet his end at the hands of his successor, Jehu, as prophesied by Elisha. It would occur in the very vineyard King Ahab stole from Naboth. Likewise Jezebel would meet her end, as would her daughter queen in Judah. For a time there would be turning away from Baal and back to the God of Israel.

There would be a generation and another and another after to fill the house in Shunem where a room had once been built upon the roof for the servant of the Lord. We had welcomed the Lord's anointed, and the Lord had returned our hospitality! We had provided a place of security for His messenger to come to rest, and God had opened my barren womb. We had lived lives of service for His messenger, and God had sent His breath to raise our son from death. We had set a table for His messenger, and God had made provision for us in the midst of our enemies during famine. We had given His messenger a seat of honor, and God had given me a place before kings.

We made room for Him. He made miracles for us.

And We Listen . . .

What a coincidence! Here is Gehazi telling the king about the Shunammite's miracles just when she and her son walk in from a seven-year sojourn! What could the king do but look at this boy who was twelve or thirteen years old now and say, "This is the child who was created in a barren womb and then raised from the dead? Okay, here is your inheritance. Take back your house, your land and, by the way, we'll pay you back rent for the past seven years."

Do you see the possibilities when you make room for the Presence? She was barren . . . her only child dead . . . facing the ravages of famine . . . her property confiscated. Yet all her needs were met.

We often focus on a particular concern and say, "I need a breakthrough here," whereas the Lord wants us to understand something more. Yes, He wants us to have that miracle, but if we stop there we will miss out. When we make room for the Presence, the balm of Gilead comes down and brings revival glory for *every* need. As carriers of the glory, we learn that one miracle is the seed for many others. Let us say it again: *A miracle from God is so magnificent each one contains within itself the life and seed for many other miracles!*

This is an important biblical principle: As we are faithful with what He gives us, He often gives us more. The more you have fellowship with Jesus, the more you are in tune with His miracle power. It is like any of the gifts. You do not walk around thinking, *I need to have a word of knowledge.* It will just be there.

The same Presence who gives discernment and prophecies and words of knowledge is not limited to one miracle.

Go Higher

The Shunammite walked in that realm of possibility. She was not thrown by each new storm. In this part of her story she returned after seven years to find her security taken over by others. There were strange people living in her house, working her land. What do they say to her? Go to the king.

What does this say to us? Go up higher.

Now here is something about going up higher: It is not about getting more complicated, more difficult, more ethereal. It is not secret knowledge. It is not for the anointed few who "really get it." The higher you go in God, the simpler things become. The anointing should be simple enough for a child to understand.

In this season, the Lord is restoring the double-portion anointing to the Church. John tells us in Revelation that he saw a new thing. The message was, "Come up, come up higher. I want to show you something." Now it is time for the Church—in our equipping and in our operation—to go to the next level.

The Church is Elisha in this hour. Elisha asked for and received a double portion of the anointing of his mentor, Elijah. Just so, we inherit from Jesus the double-portion anointing, and this enables us to breathe the living word over dead things, as Elisha did. Jesus has told us to go into all the world and preach Good News. You are His emissary, carrying the word by which the barren become fruitful and the dead things around are resurrected. He wants you to be a vessel of the double portion.

Where the Spirit of the Lord is, there is liberty, there is blessing. Your children will come home, your debts will be paid. It will be like the year of jubilee in the Bible. Many nations desperately need God to restore them. In a sense, if we do not seek revival through repentance, our children will be held in bondage to debt and loss of morality and the death of hope. Those who will not steward the double portion, who reject it and go to other gods, are going to wither. They are going to be barren, physically, economically, socially. Where the double portion is not welcome, oppression will be the outcome. The Western nations are seeing this. But there is a remedy. Wherever we welcome the name of Jesus and make room for the Holy Spirit, we will see resurrection and restoration. We will see miracles plus.

Miracles Plus

Just a few weeks ago I, Mahesh, got a desperate phone call from a pastor who is a close friend. He told me that a dear teenager in his church was in physical crisis. Her liver was failing and she was dying. A liver transplant was only a very remote possibility. He asked if I possibly had a word from the Lord about this situation.

In intercession I entered the glory, the *shekinah*, on behalf of that family and the pastor who loved them. The thick Presence of glory is almost like a bubble. Through the blood of Jesus we are allowed to enter into the double portion. Often, when we find ourselves in the midst of a challenge, we are put there to change the equation. We can enter that Presence and bring the vibration of the glory into the situation around us.

So I entered into that realm and stayed, I think, about 26 hours. I was still going about my daily business, but my spirit was engaged in the activity of heaven. I was plugged into Him, honoring His Presence and carrying this precious girl before His throne. Suddenly I emerged, and when I came out, I was with the Lord. I heard Him say, *It is done. Phone the family.* I picked up the phone and told the pastor, "It is done. The Lord said she is out of the crisis now."

The next day the doctors told the family, "This is a miracle. We don't know what changed, but she is going to live. She doesn't need a liver transplant."

Here is the thing about miracles plus. When I came out of that realm of glory, I had not only the word for her healing, but also the knowledge of the purpose that God had for her life. I told her mother to tell her daughter what the Lord had shown me about her life. This young girl had been in a lot of confusion, a crisis in her soul. In the glory was God's definition for her life and purpose. I was able to say, "This and this are her destiny."

We bless doctors. They are our friends, not enemies. But just because a doctor makes a grim diagnosis does not mean you are to accept it. You are there to change the equation, to change the atmosphere. If we believe in Jesus Christ, we can bring forth the Presence of the Holy Spirit, the *shekinah* glory, and it changes everything.

So we enter that realm not just for one miracle, the healing, but for miracles plus. It is like Hannah's story. She was praying for a child, but God had something more for her. Often we pray, "Lord, please heal me in this area," but God wants us to go beyond stage one to stage two, stage three, stage four and five. Not only did God want to give Hannah an answer to her barrenness, but also He wanted to supply Israel with a prophet, Samuel. Through her miracle child, the whole nation was blessed. In her was the seed of literally hundreds of miracles.

And think of Mary. The conception of Jesus was a miracle, and, in turn, miracles plus, for the whole sum total of all of time and place cannot contain the miracles that have and will come forth through that Child.

Whatever is coming from the Word, pick it up, enter it. The words *I am the Lord that healeth thee*, for instance, contain a whole galaxy. You can enter them and find healings for diabetes, healings for paralysis, healings for autism, healings for different kinds of cancers. The Church needs to get back into that place where we honor the Word of God. When we pray, God wants to answer our immediate problems. But He also wants to meet certain needs of the Kingdom through the answer to that prayer. He wants to give us miracles plus. We are His ambassadors of heaven. We can enter His Presence and carry a vibration of His glory that changes every equation. Ask God to help you have greater vision. You can emerge out of your trial better than you ever were, more anointed than you ever were. Just stay in the glory. God wants to take you in that situation from glory to glory.

Power in the Glory

The more you love Jesus, the more you will recognize the glory of the Lord. This glory, the thick Presence of the anointing of the Holy Spirit, gets thicker and thicker in your life as you grow in intimacy with Jesus, loving and adoring Him. There is power in the glory as it is energized by the breath of God. It depends on the deep inside of you connecting with the deep of the Lord. If you receive it, deep calls unto deep and there is an explosion of miracle power. As we behold the glory of the Lord, we are being transformed from glory to glory. God is transforming us. He is taking us from one level, wherever we are, to another level of glory.

This is the place where miracles happen. You can speak that power to a person, or a situation. You can even speak it to animals, as we have seen. If the anointing is there, you can speak it. The more you love Jesus, the more this glory will thicken.

One secret of the glory is honor. Scripture calls the honor due God the "fear of the Lord." We recognize Him as the King of glory. We love Him. We adore Him and are intimate with Him. At the same time that He is our dearest and most faithful friend, He is also the King of kings. He is our companion, but not our "buddy." Psalm 34:11 says, "Come, ye children, hearken unto me: I will teach you the fear of the Lord" (KJV). The first thing God teaches those who listen to His voice is honor for God. Modern culture has lost all sense of honor for anything. But those who would enter the glory realm where God's miracles dwell learn to hold Him, His Word, His Presence and His work in awe. Maintaining that sense of reverent wonder cultivates the atmosphere for miracles. Everything bows down in the fear of the Lord at the mention of His name.

As we make Him King in our hearts, His authority flows down and fills the atmosphere around us. If we believe that the end times are approaching, and we are surely seeing biblical fulfillment of end-time prophecies, then we must believe that Jesus, the risen Savior, the Christ, the Messiah, the Living God, the King of glory is returning soon.

This also means that the Church is going to be seen in all her glory, because the Bridegroom is coming for a Bride without spot or wrinkle in order that He might be equally yoked. So as the King of glory comes, His Bride is going to be equal in glory. The more we recognize, then, that this Bride is "us," the more we are going to want to make room for the glory of God in our hearts. This is important because this is the time when the Church will have the answers for all the needs of suffering humanity. We will have the key as Isaiah 60:1–3 (KJV) says:

> Arise, shine; for thy light is come, and the glory of the Lord is risen upon thee. For, behold, the darkness shall cover the earth,

and gross darkness the people: but the LORD shall arise upon thee, and his glory shall be seen upon thee. And the Gentiles shall come to thy light, and kings to the brightness of thy rising.

This is a prophetic word for His last-days Church. Darkness is covering the earth. There are those who call evil good and those who call good evil. But the ones who walk in the light will grow in the fruit of the Spirit, move in resurrection power and call forth miracles.

Thank God that we are being conformed into the image of Jesus! Thank God that He is dividing between flesh and spirit, between holy and unholy, between light and darkness! We welcome the rush of His Spirit, the living breath to cleanse and sanctify us that we might be a Bride without spot or blemish.

In the days to come when we face barrenness, we welcome the word that implants hope in our hearts. When our promises seem to die, we cling to the giver of life. And when earthly loss threatens to overwhelm us, we look with confidence to the King of glory. We must take the word that God gives us, even if it is a small direction, and be faithful in it. We will find in the proper times and seasons that the unction of God will be manifest in miracles of healing and in signs and wonders through us.

We are standing on the threshold of an open door. The shedding of Christ's blood has made the way for us to step into the place of miracles because of His Presence and glory. A new and living way through His blood gives us entrance to the Father's throne. Knock on the door. Enter the glory. Compel Him to come to your house. Let the promise take root in your spiritual being.

If you make room for Him to come, you will find just as the Shunammite did that the Word will come down from heaven with your miracle.

And more.

Mahesh and Bonnie Chavda have served together in full-time ministry for over thirty years, reaching the nations with the Gospel accompanied by signs and wonders. Hundreds of thousands have come to salvation, and thousands have received healing from critical diseases such as AIDS and cancer through their ministry. Many of these miracles have been medically documented, including healings of Stage IV cancer; healings of the lame, deaf and blind; and the resurrection from the dead of a six-year-old boy.

Through *The Watch* television program produced by Mahesh Chavda Ministries, Mahesh and Bonnie reach a potential audience of a billion households every week with the saving message of Jesus and are equipping believers to walk in the power and anointing of the Holy Spirit. Translated into Arabic and Farsi, *The Watch* is broadcast across the Middle East and is making a deep impact on nations within this critical region of the 10/40 window.

Mahesh and Bonnie have authored twelve books, including the Hidden Power series and *Storm Warrior*. Together the Chavdas pastor All Nations Church in Charlotte, North Carolina, and Atlanta, Georgia. They also spearhead a global prayer movement, The Watch of the Lord, where they have been leading their congregation in weekly corporate prayer for more than a decade.

Mahesh Chavda Ministries
P.O. Box 411008
Charlotte, NC 28241-1008

Phone: (704) 543-7272
Fax: (704) 541-5300

Email: info@maheshchavda.com
Website: http://www.maheshchavda.com